The Art of
Low Risk Investing

The Art of
Low Risk
Investing

Second Edition

MICHAEL G. ZAHORCHAK

VAN NOSTRAND REINHOLD COMPANY

NEW YORK   CINCINNATI   ATLANTA   DALLAS   SAN FRANCISCO
LONDON   TORONTO   MELBOURNE

Van Nostrand Reinhold Company Regional Offices:
New York Cincinnati Atlanta Dallas San Francisco

Van Nostrand Reinhold Company International Offices:
London Toronto Melbourne

Library of Congress Catalog Card Number: 77-8609
ISBN: 0-442-29577-4

Manufactured in the United States of America

Published by Van Nostrand Reinhold Company
450 West 33rd Street, New York, N.Y. 10001

Published simultaneously in Canada by Van Nostrand Reinhold Ltd.

15 14 13 12 11 10 9 8 7 6 5 4 3 2 1

Library of Congress Cataloging in Publication Data

Zahorchak, Michael G
    The art of low risk investing.

    Includes index.
    1. Investments.   2. Stocks.   I. Title.
HG4527.Z33 1977   332.6'78   77-8609
ISBN 0-442-29577-4

To my witty and whimsical sidekick

Contents

PART VII
WHAT MAKES YOU, <u>YOU</u>

Part VIII
THIS AND THAT
MISCELLANEOUS OBSERVATIONS ON
THE BUSINESS OF INVESTING

ACKNOWLEDGMENTS

I would like to acknowledge and thank the following people for their assistance in the preparation of this volume.

For permission to use the charts illustrating this book I want to thank—

Mr. R. W. Mansfield
R. W. Mansfield Co.
26 Journal Square
Jersey City, New Jersey 07306

Mr. Alan Becker
Securities Research Co.
208 Newbury Street
Boston, Massachusetts 02116

Mrs. Raynor Daniels
Trendline's Current Market Perspectives
345 Hudson Street
New York, New York 10014

Mr. Donald Worden
Worden & Worden Inc.
1915 Floranada Road
Fort Lauderdale, Florida 33308

Although the use of charts is not required when employing the Low-Risk investment method, I, like many other investors, find them to be useful for conveniently reviewing large masses of statistical data relating to a stock. The four firms whose charts are used in this book provide fine quality, accurate charts at reasonable prices in a variety of formats to suit the preferences, and varying needs of different investors. Some but not all of the formats they publish are shown in this book. A brief letter to any of these publishers will bring additional information.

I wish also to thank Louis H. Whitehead for the surgical deftness of his perceptive comments as he edited the manuscript keeping in mind the value of the ideas presented and Alberta Gordon for her valued editorial assistance in polishing up the rough edges. To my wife for her patience in first typing, then retyping many times over the manuscript to bring it to its finished form goes another acknowledgment.

My association with the American Stock Exchange does not imply that the Exchange endorses this or any other approach to the challenge of successful investing, because in fact they do not. It is left to the reader to decide for himself the merits of my observations and to apply whatever preliminary tests he feels are necessary before adopting this approach to his personal investment program.

M.G.Z.

INTRODUCTION

Many voices cry out purporting to be concerned about the welfare of the small investor. This book goes one step further. This book shows that investor how to look out for himself, because no matter how much anyone else may want to help or be in a position to help, no one can know as well as the investor himself what is best for him.

No matter where the investor looks, he has no trouble finding people ready and willing (though not always able) to look out for what they claim are his best financial interests. At work he is encouraged to have a portion of each pay withheld and invested in payroll savings, his company's stock-purchase plan, mutual funds, monthly investment plans, and so on. His loyalty is appealed to in the purchase of U.S. savings bonds; his sense of security, in the purchase of certificates of deposits; his desire to get something for nothing, by offers of free gifts for opening savings accounts; his greed, by the prospect of winning a million dollars with a dollar lottery ticket; his fear of inflation, by the purchase of stocks; and on it goes.

Not only is the investor continuously romanced by his suitors, but they often go to great pains to disparage their competitors. When the stock market is falling, savings banks remind you of the risks of owning stocks. When inflation is rampant, brokers dazzle potential investors with statistics showing that savings accounts amount to a guaranteed way of losing purchasing power. One securities salesman will convince a new investor to buy "blue chips." Then someone else will deride blue chips in favor of growth stocks because they go up in price faster. A mutual-fund salesman will convince the investor who has learned that growth stocks can also go down that what he needs is professional management of his money. This sounds great until the investor learns to his sorrow that a professional manager is often nothing more than a small investor other investors pay to lose their money for them when they lack the confidence to do it themselves. As the investor goes from one investment alternative to another, nothing seems to work out quite the way it was theoretically supposed to and, in the confusion, the investor becomes more and more desperate.

To add to the confusion, each time the market drops, dozens of Government committees are formed to conduct investigations and pass laws that are supposed to prevent people from ever losing money again. On a more realistic, day-to-day operating basis, there are numerous stock exchange, S.E.C., city and state regulatory bodies who do oversee and regulate securities markets, banks, real-estate developments, and the like. These agencies were formed to protect investors against fraud, manipulation, theft, and other such dangers. They are successful in doing what they have set out to do. It is, of course, necessary to protect us all from the deliberate fraudulent acts of other people. But this is not the biggest problem of the individual investor, and unfortunately there are few people competent to help the investor with his problem.

The greatest losses most investors suffer in the stock market generally do not rise out of the fraudulent acts of someone else, even though this sometimes happens. The investor's biggest problem is himself, and the stupid things he does to himself. He is usually his *own* worst enemy, and the person he needs the greatest protection from is himself.

This is what this book is all about. It is an effort to show the investor what he has to do in order to come to terms with the enemy within him. It also shows him how to treat the market so that every action he takes may be soundly based, confidently made, and ultimately profitable.

The times when an investor is deliberately defrauded by someone else are rare, compared to the times when the investor deceives and therefore defrauds himself. For every dollar I've lost in the market over the years, I am reasonably confident that the loss of over 99 percent of it was due to my own stupidity. I think I was defrauded only once and the money I lost then was relatively small.

An investor defrauds himself in many ways. He deceives himself when he thinks he doesn't have to work at investing. (He may not have to work hard but there is some work involved.) He defrauds himself when he thinks he can operate without guidelines. (We will come to see that very definite guidelines are available.) He defrauds himself when he thinks he can profit on tips, inside information, or otherwise ride on someone else's coattails. Sometimes he can, but generally the price he pays for these tips comes high; tips are often circulated by investors after they buy their own stock to influence other people to push it up to where the first buyer can sell his own stock at a profit. The investor sets himself up for almost certain losses when he allows his prejudices to interfere with correct investment decisions.

The price he pays for his deceptions is always high, so high in fact that someone once estimated that over a complete stock-market cycle, only about 5 percent of all investors make any money at all. Another 15 percent manage to break even, while the remaining 80 percent lose money.

The statement appeared rather far-fetched until I read somewhere else that Internal Revenue Department records appear to support this observation. They show that even in years when the stock market is going up sharply, more people report net-capital losses than net-capital gains on their tax returns.

Another illustration of how difficult it is to make money in stocks, even when a person is right about the market, came from privately circulated figures of a large brokerage house near the end of the 1969-1970 bear market. The report showed that even those customers who as a group foresaw the bear market, and tried to take advantage of it by selling stocks short, lost money as a group because the *timing* of their short selling and their subsequent short covering was all wrong.

These figures are difficult to comprehend by anyone who has seen a chart showing the broad sweep of stock-market movements but has never invested himself. Such a study of stock prices might give one the impression that making consistent profits in the stock market should not present much of a problem. Even a casual glance at the stock-market table in a newspaper showing the range of prices for the past year will indicate that the difference between the high and low price of almost any stock during the year is at least 30 to 40 percent, while the spread between the high and low prices for literally hundreds of the more volatile stocks ranges from 100 to 500 percent or more.

With swings of this amplitude, it would appear that the odds are seemingly in your favor and that it is impossible to lose. The investor who has learned how to time these movements should be able to set a price-appreciation target for himself of at least 50 percent a year and be almost certain of achieving it. Actually, it would appear that the investor should be able to shoot for doubling his money each and every year before taxes and come close to achieving that goal. Then, if he could somehow learn to hold on to his profits during the bear-market years when almost every stock is going down, and could harness the pyramiding power of compound interest, an investor should be able to set a target for himself of over a half-million dollars in capital gains in just 10 years for each $10,000 he started with!

So while this is not a book about how to make a million dollars in a week using other people's money, it is intended to show what it takes to make a million over a period of years when one starts with a modest initial investment, and then what it takes to keep the million from slipping through your fingers.

There is a price, though, and you have to be willing to pay it. To achieve the kind of results we are talking about, the investor must be willing to learn a little about how he functions; he must not be afraid to discipline himself; and he must not mind spending five to ten hours each week on his investments, thereby treating them as a serious business undertaking rather than as a fling at the race track or at a gaming table.

How to go about this is what we are going to talk about, and the manner in which we are going to talk about it is what makes this book so different from any other book on investing you have ever read. The most important element in achieving investment success does not reside in any secret system that you might stumble upon. Instead, the most important single element in the investment equation at all times is you, the individual investor, and what you are doing in relation to the market, regardless of what the market itself is doing. Because this is true, we are going to spend most of our time in the second half of the book talking about you, and what you have to do to achieve consistent success in the marketplace.

In the first part of the book, we will study specific investment techniques—techniques which are not new in themselves, but which have a unique application different from anything you may have seen in the past.

Indeed, rather than complicate the problem, we are going in the other extreme. The objective will be to learn how to work with the simplest, least-complicated tools possible. You will soon see that one of your problems in the past may have been caused by unnecessarily complicating what is essentially a very simple procedure, for all an investor really needs to be successful is the ability to observe and use a few simple tools and a few simple rules.

These simple techniques may be lacking in glamour, but fortunately they more than make up for it in results that are reason enough to adopt them. With these tools, the investor can achieve for himself a better, more-consistent record of performance than virtually any professional has ever turned in on his behalf. We are shooting for a profit target of 100 percent a year, but if we just make and keep a small portion of this, most of us will still find ourselves with better results than we have ever known.

Once you have become oriented to the techniques in this book, you will find them easier to use than any others you have used before. The re-orientation will involve an affirmative resolution to make your own investment decisions, because you will know more about what is good for you than anyone else can know. You will need to learn how to operate in the market with an open mind. *You've got to be able to accept things as they are rather than as they ought to be.* This is no easy chore. It is, in fact, one of the toughest things in the world. When you start to think for yourself, there are times when you invariably find yourself reaching conclusions different from those you've made before, what you've read in the papers, or the opinions of your friends. At first you will find yourself all alone in left field, and it will be lonely out there.

You will want to come back into the grandstand with the crowd because it is always more comfortable being part of a crowd. But the cruel fact is that the stock market will rarely—if ever profitably—accommodate a crowd. Generally, the price of being gregarious is extremely high, so high that the price of following the crowd is not just the loss of some theoretically potential profit but of the money that was put in for investment to begin with.

The pity of it all is that it doesn't have to happen that way. Each man has built into him a natural instinct for survival and this instinct is crying out to be used, though most of us choose to ignore it. Every man who ever fought in a war, and everyone who ever successfully survived a crisis in his life, knows about that instinct but only a few people know how to go about using it on a day-in, day-out basis.

The stock market is an ideal place to learn to use this instinct constructively. The constructive use of instinct in the market, in conjunction with a good market system, by even the most inexperienced investor will protect his investment and make it grow beyond anything he has experienced. Actually the correct use of this instinct will at times be more important in achieving the really big stock-market profits than any information, advice, or techniques the investor can get from any outer source.

More people probably lose more money because they use too much information incorrectly than they would if they didn't bother with any information at all. It doesn't matter here what kind of information we are talking about, whether the "too much" includes facts about the company, its operations, knowledge that "they" are going to push the stock up, or whatever. If we know and use even good information improperly or at the wrong time, we can suffer a bigger loss than we might without any such information at our disposal in the first place. When you get right down to the heart of it, the only question an investor has to answer for himself is this: "If I buy this stock right now, at this moment, at this price, will I be able to sell it on some future tomorrow at some higher price?" Then, if he knows what to look for and the answer is yes or probably so, he buys; if the answer is no or probably not, he ignores the stock. It's that simple.

So this, too, is what this book is about. It's about the individual peculiarities of you and me and everyone else. It's about why we have these peculiarities and hang-ups; how we got them in the first place; how they help or hurt us; and how we can go about either changing them or at least suppressing those that hurt us most in the market.

We will now go on to a very simple system for consistently making stock-market profits. The techniques differ from most others in that they are designed to show when to buy at times when the risk of capital loss is small, as well as to point out which stocks show potential for high capital gains. If, instead of the losses you have had in the past, you could have broken even (or almost so) and held on to the profits you had, think of how much better your overall investment results would be.

We will show you the tools you will need and how to use them to achieve consistently profitable results on balance. Because it is impossible to design an absolutely perfect system, you will not, even with this system, make a profit on every stock you buy. You can, however, learn to have more profitable trades more often than ever before, and you can learn to keep your losses down while you let your profits run. We will show you how to do this.

In the stock market, the way people act and react is really the name of the game. That's the exciting part of it. Everything else is just there to confuse the real issue. How they think; how they act, and why they do the things they do is where it's at. If you can understand this—nothing else—you will know almost all you need to know about what makes prices move up and down. If you know how and why you act the way you do, you know almost all you need to know to make and keep any bull market's profits. Almost any market will in fact become a bull market for you. You won't have to fear bear markets, because for you there will never be a bear market—only times when stocks are cheap and crying to be bought, and times when stocks are high and not worth holding any longer.

The Art of
Low Risk Investing

PART I

Where Do You Start?

1. You've Got to Start Somewhere

Obviously, if you are going to become a successful investor, you've got to start somewhere. In fact, if you are to become any sort of investor, successful or not, you've still got to start someplace. The problem is, where do you start?

If it is really true that only 5 percent of those who invest in the market are consistently successful while 80 percent of us consistently lose, this is a frightening statistic, and all the more so because of what some of the implications behind these statistics might infer. It suggests, for instance, that there are so few successful investors because:

1. The people who make all the money in the market are smarter than the rest of us.
2. They are on the pipe line to more inside information than the rest of us.
3. They are all crooks who manipulate the market for their own convenience and fleece the rest of us of our money.

I was not willing personally to concede to the thesis that intelligence is a criteria of investment success. In fact, I was egotistic enough to believe there is no correlation between intelligence and investment success. In graduate school, I got a master's degree in investments and economics, along with an award for the best average in the investments major. Nevertheless, for years, my investment results were mediocre at best.

On the other hand, the most successful investor I know of probably never bought a single share of stock in his life. All he did was inherit and hold on to one of the most fabulously successful stocks of all time. This man is a telephone repairman who when a baby was given a couple of hundred shares of a stock no one remembers today but which later, through either merger or some changes in name, has become familiar to us as I.B.M. Over the years, with its numerous stock splits and stock dividends, his investment has come to be worth several million dollars— all because this man was never tempted as he went along to take his profits and get into something with "better assured growth prospects."

From time to time, I've met other successful investors. Most of them are shy, quiet, soft-spoken. While invariably intelligent, they are probably no more intelligent than you or most of your friends and they are just as likable and easy to get along with. The really intellectual people in Wall Street are not necessarily the ones who make the big profits from trading stocks. The geniuses in Wall Street are the lawyers, underwriters, accountants, mutual-fund managers, and the others who make their money from the big fees they charge for their services, and from the stock that their clients often give them free or at very little cost. When it comes to personal investing, however, they do not necessarily do any better than the rest of us.

It is no big trick to make money in the stock market if someone gives you for $5 a share a stock that is selling at $20 a share today. It is a lot more difficult to make money in the market buying a stock in the open market that is selling at $5 today in order to sell it as $20 a year or so from today.

So, intelligence by itself will not determine how well or how poorly you will perform as an investor. Never count yourself either in or out of the game on this account. If you are highly intelligent, this in itself will not guarantee that you will make money in the market. Similarly, even if you are of less-than-average intelligence, this does not preclude you from making stock-market profits. If that is what you are determined to do, the fact of the matter is that you can do just that.

The next factor we have to consider is inside information. It might seem reasonable to believe that, since those people who do make money consistently in the market probably do know something you don't know, that something has to be inside information. This does not necessarily follow. The case of Penn Central stock, which is described later in this book, refutes this theory. You may recall that directors of Penn Central came under investigation in 1970 for possible criminal prosecution when they allegedly sold their stock at $18 a share several weeks before the railroad planned to file for bankruptcy. As unfair as this might seem, a small investor without any inside information whatever but armed with the techniques in this book would have been able to sell his Penn Central stock a full year and a half earlier at $69 a share, thus netting himself a profit 283 percent greater than he would have received had he been on the Penn Central pipe line, waiting for the directors to tell him when to sell the stock! And the beauty of all this is that he could have achieved these results without even knowing what business Penn Central was in.

I've met any number of corporate officers who observed that they did not understand the market because as often as not, when the corporation announced good news, its stock would go down in price; then, when it announced bad news and expected its stock to fall, often it went up instead. A corporate director, astute in the ways of the market, once said he did not think more than one director in a hundred could correctly guess how a stock might react to a specific announcement at a specific time.

Many stock-exchange specialists who are among the minority of successful investors go out of their way not to hear any information until after it has been released on the news wires. They reason that so much information is distributed that never affects investors one way or another, so the only news they need pay any attention to is the kind that has "grabbed" investors to the point where it is making them buy or sell stocks.

So inside information isn't the answer to stock-market success. Most of the time it has no effect on the price of a stock. When it does have an effect, and you are an insider who is caught using it, you stand to lose not only your profits but you may receive a fine and a prison sentence as well. So if you are not on a pipe line to any inside information, don't spend your time thinking of ways to get piped in. You don't need it. It cannot always help you, and it can hurt.

It is possible that the information you get will probably not be good. For example, some time ago, I was involved in an investigation of a stock. Manipulation was suspected. The stock was so much in the limelight that during the course of the investigation over two hundred people wrote letters to my employer about the stock. Many of the correspondents named persons that they alleged were involved in manipulating the stock. Among all these letters and all the people they mentioned, only three listed the names of anyone either directly or even remotely connected with the stock at that time. Over half the people named in the letters had never so much as bought or sold one share of stock, while the remainder were involved with only a few hundred of the thousands of shares that were traded.

This leads right into the question of deliberate fraud. *It is not realistic to think that everyone in the market or that everyone "but me" is a crook.* It is not only unrealistic but unhealthy from a psychological standpoint. We will have more to say on this later. It is sufficient to say at this point that there are indeed people who do try to manipulate a stock from time to time. But this happens less often than you might suppose. Nevertheless, as you will see, this is not necessarily your problem; nor should you overly concern yourself if you are operating with good guidelines. The stock exchanges and the S.E.C. have excellent people tracking down the criminals operating in the market. It may take some time but they eventually catch them all, if the market, in its superb equalizing fashion, doesn't take care of them first.

The fact that there are manipulators in the market will not necessarily hurt you. They might even help, because if they successfully manipulate a stock you own, you might make a bigger profit than would otherwise be the case. Just as the Good Lord is supposed to be especially tolerant of drunks and children, the market can be very tolerant of your ignorance if, in your ignorance, you innocently get involved on the right side of a manipulated stock. Of course, with our approach *you will learn never to be on the wrong side of any stock, manipulated or not.* Your only possible problem will come if you learn about the manipulation and then let greed persuade you to deviate from your market approach in this special case in favor of the stories you have heard.

So here we are. We know we have to start somewhere, and we've learned your intelligence doesn't have all that much to do with how well you perform as an investor. If you are fairly intelligent, you will soon learn not to become too egotistic because the market can humble a person more completely than anything else. On the other hand, if you believe yourself to be not too bright, don't despair. As I've said earlier, it doesn't take brains to make money in the market; lots of people prove this all the time.

We know also that you don't need to be on any kind of inside track to make money in the market, because sometimes the information you get wouldn't have any effect or at other times an effect exactly opposite of what was anticipated. So, if you can't depend on it, there is no need to have it.

Also we have to believe that not all successful investors are crooks, and that this doesn't make any difference, anyway; if there are crooks, they won't be able to touch us once we know how to reduce stock-market risk.

2. Fundamentals as a Key to Stock-Market Profits

The next logical place to look for the key to stock-market profits is in the area of fundamentals. We must have sufficient information about a company before we can make an intelligent investment decision. After all, if a stock goes up or down, there has to be a reason for it, and if you know enough about the company, it seems you should then know what that reason is.

This sounds sensible and logical except for three factors: First, there are practical problems involved in accumulating information. There is often so much information available about a company, and it is so widely scattered, that you can't get your hands on all of it. Next, if you are missing some facts, your ignorance of them can very well be the key to the success or failure of your investment. Finally, when you do get all your information together and make a judgment about what a stock should do, you will find that as often as not the stock will do something contrary to what a rational review of the facts would lead you to believe.

At such times, knowing what a stock should be doing can be more dangerous than operating in complete ignorance. For instance, if you bought a stock that is supposed to be going up but is going down instead, you will probably decide to hold on to that stock. As you watch your loss get bigger and bigger, you are likely to be like the man standing out on a prairie who looked up to see a herd of cattle stampeding toward him. Instead of getting the hell out of the way of the stampede as fast as he could, he just stood there shouting, "Hey, what are you doing coming this way? Don't you know you're supposed to be going the other way?"

The first and foremost problem in dealing with information today is that there is just too much of it. The problem is so acute that we have reams of statistical information around just to inform us that we are in the midst of the greatest information explosion in history. Statistics tell us the amount of new information available in the world is doubling every twenty-five years. Some years ago, while working for a brokerage house, I was inundated with several hundred pages of research reports, wire flashes, news announcements, industry reviews, etc., each day. In self-defense it eventually became necessary to ignore them all completely. It was a case of mental indigestion—my mind just couldn't assimilate all the information it was being fed, so I went on a diet. I found it possible to operate more effectively by referring to research reports only when needed than by reading indiscriminately everything that was being written.

Almost every company of any size has at least one person on its payroll whose primary job is to communicate with investors or with people who can influence investors. His success is measured by his ability to keep the company's name in the public eye. When there is nothing significant to announce, it is his job to manufacture something to say just so the name of his company is kept before investors.

This is all well and good, but if you base an investment approach on this kind of information, you will soon find yourself hopelessly bogged down. There is so much information available that you cannnot possibly begin to read all of it. You run therefore, a continuous risk of missing news that can be significant to you in making your investment decision.

As for the information you do read, you will find that much of it is manufactured news without any bearing on any investment decision you might have to make, and that any time you spend reading it will have been time wasted.

When you finally get down to some statistics you can sink your teeth into, you may find that you have no really satisfactory guidepost against which to measure these statistics. For instance, one of the basic fundamental tools of an analyst is the price-earnings ratio of a stock. On the surface of it, this looks like an excellent tool to use. All a person has to know is that when the ratio is low the stock is a buy, and when it is high it should be sold. This is simple enough except that no one has ever been satisfactorily able to explain how low is low, how high is high, and how you can figure out what is just right for now.

For example look at the four charts in Figure 1. These charts show the price range by week for a three-and-one-half year period. The two more-or-less parallel dotted lines that bracket the ranges are price-earnings ratio lines. Trendline, who publishes these charts, states that their research has shown that most stocks with continuous and relatively stable earnings have a tendency to trade within these ranges in relation to their earnings. If you look at the first stock, Supermarkets General Corp., you will see that the stock has normally traded between 9 and 23 times earnings. Therefore, if the stock that was last trading at about $25 were to trade at $42, it would be trading at 23 times then-prevailing earnings; if it sold at $17, it would be trading at 9 times currently prevailing earnings. The difference between $17 and $42 is $25 or almost 150 percent of the lower $17 price. This means that the stock could trade anywhere between $17 and $42 and still be considered normally priced.

Even this information might be useful if we could assume that the stock would always trade within these parameters. Then all one has to do is buy the stock when it gets down near the bottom line, or its low P/E ratio, and sell when its gets to the top. But note that in 1968 when Supermarkets sold at $22 it never got to within 4 points of the top of the range. Therefore, if you had waited for the stock to hit the top of the range before selling instead of taking a nice profit, you would have found yourself holding the stock all the way down to $8 in 1970. Instead of finding the courage to buy more stock because it was now at the low end of its historical price range, you probably would have been frightened out of your wits enough to sell the stock at a loss instead.

Now look at the variations you can get to complicate the problem:

1. First, the price-earnings ratio ranges for each stock are different. In this one illustration alone, the low P/E ranges from 10 to 20 while the

high end of the range goes from 20 to 65. A professional working with these ratios full time might be able to make some sense out of what is supposed to constitute normality, but it is beyond the comprehension of many other professionals and most nonprofessional investors.

2. Note that by definition the range lines will disappear should the company show a loss, because then it would have no earnings around which to build a range. Under these circumstances, an investor relying on earnings as his guidepost would be left without any to follow.

3. Some stocks don't seem to hit either the top or the bottom of their ranges for years at a time.

4. When a stock does get to the top of its P/E range, it does not follow that it will bounce off and head down. Look at the chart for Swift & Co. Here the P/E line was turning down sharply in 1968. Instead of the stock hitting this line and turning down with it, the price of Swift went up through the line and traded above it for almost a full year.

5. When a stock gets down to the bottom of its normal P/E range, again it does not follow that the stock will "base out" here and start to move higher in price. Syntex hit the bottom of its P/E line at $44 in January, 1970, but instead of turning around and moving up, it fell more than 50 percent down to under $20 in July of the same year.

6. There is no consistent and readily acceptable formula available regarding the construction of this P/E ratio range. Different analysts will have different ideas of what "normal" is supposed to mean.

7. Finally, over a period of years, the concept of what is normal changes. Until about 1950 anything above about 15 or 20 times earnings was considered abnormally high. Then, by the late 1960's, investors became used to seeing stocks sell at 30, 40, even 60 times earnings. Just as this became accepted as the new norm, stocks skid in a series of two bear markets in 1970 and again in 1974. Toward the end of 1974, the average P/E ratio was about 7.5 with the stocks of hundreds of fine companies down to four or less.

You can see from this that while price-earnings ratios might be of some value to a person setting up the boundaries of the ball park in which he is going to play the investment game, they are really of no help to him when he zeroes in on precisely when to buy or sell.

Another kind of statistics many investors like to use is the rate-of-earnings growth. According to this theory, all you have to do is find a stock whose earnings are growing and one of these days, just as sure as you are reading this book, the stock is going to move up in price in line with the growth in earnings. On the other hand, if you find a stock that is losing money, you can be equally sure that the stock is going to fall in

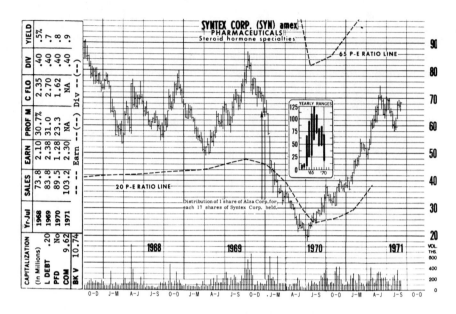

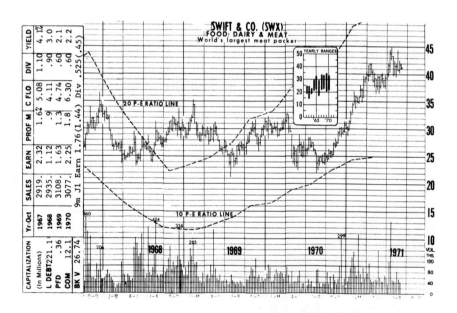

Figure 1   *(Courtesy Trendline's Current Market Perspectives)*

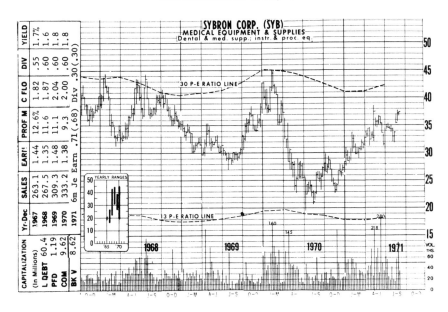

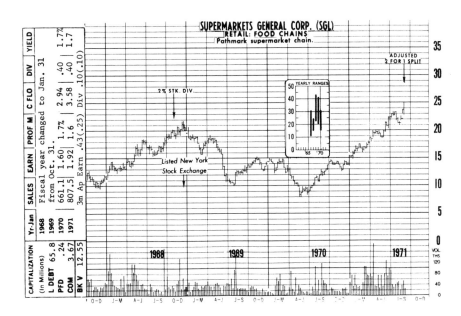

Figure 1 (Continued)

price. This, too, seems logical and it makes sense, except that the many exceptions to the rule make the rule invalid.

For instance, look at the chart of Washington Water Power Co. (Figure 2). The solid line with dots on it shows the earnings level of the stock read from the scale on the left. Note the almost uninterrupted growth of earnings achieved by the company. Yet, in August, 1974, when the company was earning $2.15 per share, the stock dipped under $16. On the highest earnings in eleven years, the stock was selling at its lowest price in eleven years.

On the other hand, look at the Denny's Inc. chart (Figure 3). It shows that in 1969, earnings dropped slightly from 80 cents per share to about 65 cents and the stock started to fall. The price continued to fall even when earnings recovered. Then, in the third quarter of 1970, the stock hit a low of $5¾ just as earnings were peaking. For the next year, as earnings declined, the stock did not drop any lower. All through 1972 both earnings and the price of the stock rose, but in 1973 and 1974, as earnings continued to rise, the price of the stock fell from over $20 to under $6.

Lest the reader think this kind of performance was limited to just these two stocks, ponder the performance of all stocks in 1974 and 1975. For business, 1974 was a banner year. By October 31, the average company on the New York Stock Exchange reported an increase in

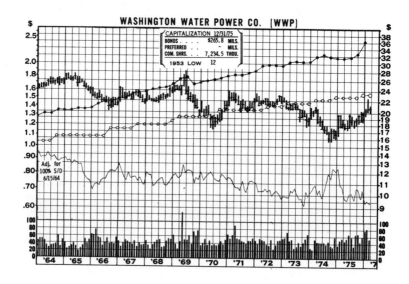

Figure 2

earnings of 21 percent but the price of the average stock was 33 percent lower than it was a year earlier. Then in 1975, the opposite happened: earnings were down 14 percent while stock prices rose an average of 33 percent.

If you wanted to go on, you could find dozens of other criteria that could become factored into the investment equation. All these criteria are important pieces of information, nice to know, but to the best of my

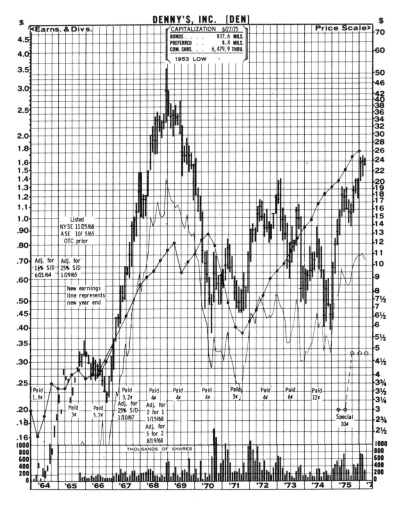

Figure 3

knowledge none of them have the consistency for use with confidence in a programmable stock-market system.

Therefore, while we do have to find something to use as our standard of value, fundamental information does not seem to be the answer. You can never be sure you've read enough about a specific company; you can never be sure you are even reading about the right company. Invariably, you will learn after the fact that a company with the best peformance of all will be one that you have overlooked, never even heard of, or discarded as not worth owning.

If you have studied the right company, you may very likely have decided it was not worth owning, only to read a short time later of the big move it made. Or, you will decide it is already overpriced when there is still much more potential profit left. Or, you will buy a stock with strong fundamentals that just sits there for years on end and does nothing at all.

3. Charts and Technical Tools as Keys to Stock-Market Profits

While fundamentals do have their shortcomings, they nevertheless are important. Most investors do and properly should use them as a basis for determining which stocks they will consider as potential invest-ments. Fundamentals then serve as an initial screening device to narrow the potential list of selections down to more manageable levels. We, too, will use fundamentals in our low-risk approach as part of a series of screening devices for making our selections, but our screening devices will be of a different, simpler variety from those used by the fundamentalists.

Many of the more professional investors narrow down their selection of potential-purchase candidates, and then turn to stock charts to try to time the purchase and sale of their investments. When you get involved in a study of charts, you have to contend with such things as trend lines, head and shoulders, triangles, saucers, gaps, and dozens of other formations. These chart patterns and formations are supposed to contain predictive characteristics for the future, based on the implica-tions of the particular pattern that is being formed.

There are all sorts of arguments around as to whether the charts really can portend future price movements, or whether—now that so many investors know chart theory—there is a tendency to make certain obvious chart forecasts self-fulfilling. If the arguments are valid it doesn't really matter. The conclusions to be drawn from the fact that the argument exists at all are that charts may be valuable and that they may help achieve investment profits. Anyone who has used them for any length of time does know they help improve investment results.

But they do have their disadvantages. The principal disadvantage stems from the very nature of a chart. A stock chart is nothing more than a pictorial representation of how the price of the stock was traced in the past in response to the opposing forces at work in the market of that stock. Because it is a story of the past, an investor studying a chart cannot always judge successfully how a pattern that seems to be evolving at the present time is going to resolve itself until after the pattern has been completed. Upon the completion of an evolving pattern, a stock sometimes moves so fast in the direction indicated that most—if not all—the indicated profit is lost to the investor who is even slightly slow in reacting to it.

An even more basic problem is that interpreting charts is much more an art than it is a science. In this respect, it must be a lot like what divining the future by means of reading chicken entrials must have been when that sort of thing was in vogue. If you ask a dozen chartists to interpret a chart for you while it is in the process of evolving, you will get a dozen different ideas of what they think the stock is likely to do. In the process, if you are observant you will learn a lot about the personalities of the respective analysts, but very little that will help you decide whether to buy or sell the stock. This is what makes chart reading much more an art than a science, and for this reason, it becomes too imprecise for use by at least as many investors as it helps.

A final difficulty, and the biggest disadvantage of charts, stems from the fact that invariably they do not work at precisely the times they are needed the most, namely when the market is putting the finishing touches to a major top or bottom. At market bottoms, almost every chart pattern will seem bearish and appear to point to a much, much lower level of prices. At market tops, the reverse is true; almost every chart looks bullish and shows promise of huge profits that will not be fulfilled.

Charts, then, are most helpful during the long middle periods of bull and bear markets. Modifying their usefulness, they are often dangerous and will produce losses at major turning points for even those experienced in their use. If you have the time and inclination to learn to use charts as something more than a pictorial reference of past history, by all means do so. But just remember their limitations.

4. Moving Averages as Keys to Stock-Market Profits

Another major school of analysis employs various kinds of mathematical calculations. The techniques we will be using as the keystone of our investment system center around the use of so-called "moving averages." In addition to moving averages, there are dozens of other techniques and tools that serve to help, hinder, or merely confuse the investor in his search for profits. Some people study shifts in the money supply and credit. Others study statistics designed to measure the psychological state of investors. Still others work with various means for measuring momentum. They work with computers, use game theory, evolve statistical distributions and theories as involved as it is possible for the mind to create.

Significantly, one of the simplest stock-market systems created, the one presented in this book, will work almost as well as the best of these more complicated methods at their best, and much better than the rest—regardless of how sophisticated the method. Furthermore, our system doesn't require any mathematical knowledge beyond grade-school arithmetic. All mathematical systems eventually break down into simple arithmetic. A moving average as we will use it is a valuable tool that will serve us as the anchor or guideline we are looking for, against which we will be able to judge the constantly fluctuating price process that occurs in every stock.

The significance of these continual price changes is often overlooked and misinterpreted, unless the investor can find some standard against which they can be judged. For instance, a person might read in the paper that a stock fell four points today and become concerned about it. But, if he recalls that this same stock went up ten points last week, the four-point drop may be nothing more than a necessary correction that occurs whenever the market goes too far in either direction.

Likewise, the papers might say the market was up strongly today, but if the Dow Jones had just dropped a hundred points in the last few weeks, the strength in the market might be just a corrective breather that comes before a further drop.

Moving averages are generally of certain specified time periods. For instance, we will work with three different averages—5, 15, and 40 weeks in length. The beauty of a moving average is that it provides within the framework of a fixed period of time the correct anchor value against which to judge each stock in relation to its own market performance.

In case you are unfamiliar with a moving average, it is a middle number or an arithmetic mean of a series of consecutive numbers. For instance, if for five consecutive Friday afternoons the price at which a stock traded was 20, 21, 19, 18, and 22, then the total of these five numbers would be 100 and the average would be 20. To get the average, it is only necessary to add the numbers, then divide the total—100 in this case—by the number of weeks involved—which are 5—to get the average price, or 20.

A moving average is exactly the same as a regular average except that it "moves" because it is being continuously updated as new data becomes available. In our case, this would be at the end of each week as a new closing price for each successive Friday is posted. Because each week's updated average price generally differs slightly from the average of the preceding week as the stock moves either up or down in price, the average is said to "move" in response to these price fluctuations.

The precise manner of constructing a moving average, along with our rules for using them, will be explained in detail later.

As with other techniques, there are drawbacks to the use of moving averages. The biggest disadvantage I find in this standard moving-average theory is related to the difficulty I have with charts generally. Although the moving average is a more precise device than any chart, it still has a tendency at times to make an investor somewhat vulnerable to swift market declines, especially at market tops when a stock might crack almost without notice. By the time the average gives a sell signal, a huge portion of an investor's profits are lost. This occurs because prices seem to generally fall about twice as fast as they rise. An effective system, therefore, has to factor this into its equation. It has to allow an investor to remain invested for the full duration of a stock's rise, then permit him to withdraw quickly when the rise is completed.

Another disadvantage is that the moving-average technique does not work well with some types of stocks. With some stocks, it produces, instead of the profits we hope to see, a series of small "whipsaw" losses.

We will learn to recognize those stocks that are not likely to work well under our system, and to avoid any consideration of them as possible investment candidates.

The moving average as *we will use it* will provide us with a precise tool for timing specifically *when* a stock should be bought and specifically *when* it should be sold. *At the time* we make our purchases, we may not know how high the stock is likely to move or even why it is going to make its move. In fact, at the time we get our signals to buy a stock, much of the news and information about the stock may be negative. To our broker and our friends, we will seem fools for buying the stock. Yet, as we shall see, future events will bear out the fact that our purchases had been made at precisely the right time. At the time of our purchases, the risk of losing any substantial amount of money will be limited, while the prospect for profits will often be in the magnitude of several hundred to several thousand percent.

Conversely, at the *time* our signals will tell us to sell, everything we read about the company will be screaming, "Hold on to the stock. Don't sell. If anything, buy more." Yet this will be just the time that the risk of ownership will be the greatest. While others will be influenced by what they are reading in the papers, you will be influenced and acting on the basis of what the stock itself is telling you to do.

5. Price—the Resolution of All Forces

By emphasizing a system based on moving averages, we will be emphasizing a system based on price alone. We shall not abandon fundamentals in our initial research, but once a decision has been made that we are willing to buy a stock when the price is right, our effort will then be turned almost exclusively to following price actions.

A successful system for buying and selling stocks can be based on price and nothing else because in the end price is the ultimate resolution of all the forces that have an effect on any particular stock at any particular time. Everything anybody knows, thinks, believes, or feels about a stock is translated into the price at which a stock trades. If an investor sees a stock selling at $10 that he believes is worth $20 right now, and if he wants to take advantage of this difference in price, he will start buying the stock—and will continue buying it until either the price runs up to $20 or he runs out of money.

On the other hand, if someone else who owns that same stock thinks it is worth less than $10, he is happy to see this buyer on the scene; he now has someone he can aggressively sell his stock to. When these two opposing forces meet head-on, the stock will remain at $10 until the buyer either runs out of money or the seller runs out of stock. If the buyer runs out of money first, the stock will never get above $10. If the reverse is true, the seller is soon likely to scold himself for having sold too soon.

One advantage of using an investment system based purely on price comes from the self-evident fact that the less you have to pay for a stock at any particular time, the better a relative bargain it is. Because the aim of the game is to buy low and sell high, our moving-average technique automatically calculates for us the best relative level at which to buy and the best relative level at which to sell.

To visualize how this is done, glance at the chart of Rowan Corp. (Figure 4). The numbers that appear on Rowan chart above and below the weekly price ranges represent the Price-Earnings ratio of the stock at the time of each posting. If earnings remain the same while a stock is moving up in price, the ratio of the price to earnings will increase. If the price declines, the P-E ratio will also drop.

In actual practice what often happens is that as earnings increase the price goes up more than earnings. Then, as earnings decrease, the price shrinks much more than the drop in earnings would appear to warrant. Both conditions are illustrated in the chart. As Rowan's earnings increased on a cumulative basis from $1.96 to $2.06 a share, the stock went from about $34 a share to $60 and its P-E ratio rose from 17.4 to 30.3. Then as the earnings fell to $1.42 a share, the P-E ratio also dropped from the high of 30.3 to a low of 7.6.

Week after week, the moving average of Rowan's price reflected this change in evaluation by first rising and then falling as the opposing forces in the market first pushed Rowan's price up and then drove it down.

By "signaling" the purchase of Rowan at about $15 a share after the decline from $60, the moving average automatically resolved for the investor all the questions he might have had about when to buy the stock—and did so without making him resort to the infinitely more complex means of seeking out all the available information on the company.

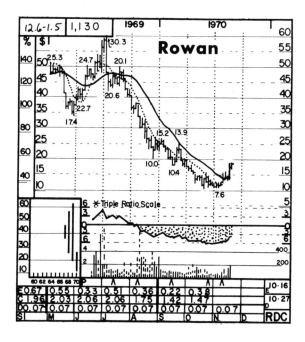

Figure 4 *(Courtesy R. W. Mansfield Co.)*

PART II

Cycles – Round and Round They Go

6. Theory of Market and Emotional Cycles

Investors and other students of the market ultimately come to the realization that stock prices do not always (or even often) reflect the values inherent in the company represented by that stock. Instead the price level of a particular stock, or of the stock market in general, is to a very large degree a measure of the overall emotional attitude of investors at a specific moment of time toward a specific stock or the overall stock market. It is a measure of how people choose to look at the values represented by the stock and, more specifically, *what they choose to do about these values*. It is this intensity with which people choose to act that determines how high or how low the price level of any stock will go.

When people are overly enthusiastic, they bid stocks to levels so high that they can be neither justified nor maintained. Therefore, such high prices are generally temporary and the stocks soon fall to more reasonable levels. When people are overly pessimistic, their selling drives prices down too low. This, too, is temporary and the price ultimately recovers. Peaks and valleys of emotion in the stock market, as in individual people, cannot be maintained indefinitely. When prices get too far out of line, sooner or later the emotional changes of people swing them back into what is a more normal level. It has been thought that the movement of stock prices is random and unpredictable but this is not so. *Over an extended period of time, the stock market moves in waves that can readily be observed by even a cursory inspection of any chart of stock movements.*

These alternating waves of changing emotion cause prices to move first up, then down, above and below the theoretical value of stocks, even when there is no fundamental change in the outlook of a company. Look at the chart showing the price fluctuations of the Dow-Jones averages from 1914 through 1970 (Figure 5). If you look carefully, you can see a regular pattern of clearly defined market bottoms. In recent years they have occured about every four years (if you don't want to get too fussy about the precise number of days or months from one bottom to the next).

Working back, there was an identifiable market bottom in 1974, 1970, 1966, 1962, 1958, 1953, 1949, 1946, 1942, 1938, 1932, 1929, 1926, 1923, 1921, 1917, and 1914. This averages out to about 51 months between major identifiable bottoms for the period from 1932 to 1974, and 36 months between bottoms for the period from 1914 through 1932.

The Foundation for the Study of Cycles in Pittsburgh, Pennsylvania, published a catalog several years ago that summarized the results of hundreds of attempts by dozens of researchers to isolate cycles of various lengths, not only in the stock market but in numerous other areas as well. These researchers reported finding in a time span from 48 to 59 months a cluster of 24 different cycles (or perhaps it was the same cycle measured differently, thus producing slightly different results). Another cluster of cycles was noted in a 14-to-17-week zone while dozens of others were isolated in various time periods ranging from 22 weeks to 22 months.

What causes these patterns, we do not know, but we can see visually that they do exist, and we can use this knowledge as one of the elements in our successful investment program. How this is done will be shown shortly.

The market is random from minute to minute because the influence that causes a stock to trade is the willingness of an investor to call his broker with an order to either buy or sell stock at the market. The term, "at the market," means that an investor is willing to accept the best available price at the time he enters his order. If he is a buyer, that price is either the same or a fraction of a point higher than the last recorded price. If he is a seller, then the price would be either the same or a fraction of a point lower than the last recorded price. Since over 30 million people own stocks, it is impossible to know at any particular time which investor will enter the next order in any stock, and it is just as impossible to know whether he will choose to buy or sell. So from this short-term point of view the market is random.

It is possible, however, to estimate at any specific time the emotional state of the total body of investors, and to thereby judge whether more people are likely to buy or sell causing the market to go up or down. We can do this because people's emotions regularly alternate between optimism or pessimism within time periods that we can measure. To the degree that this happens regularly, the stock market is cyclical and predictable.

Emotional cycles occur in people individually and in humanity as a group. The individual emotional cycle is approximately 28 days long, while one of the longer-term cycles meaningful to investors oriented toward capital gains appears, as we have seen, to last about four to four

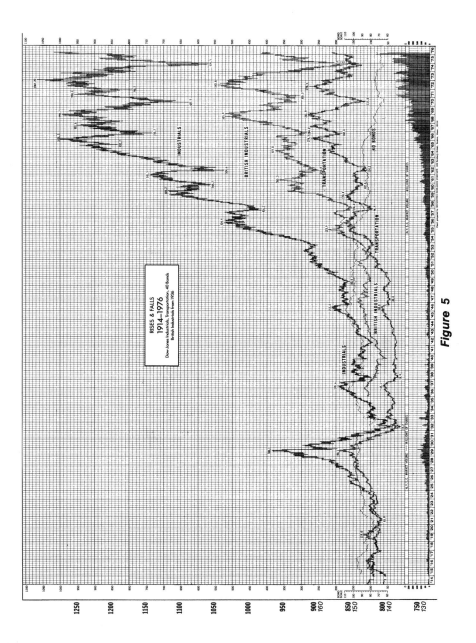

Figure 5

and-one-half years. For an idea of a typical cycle, look at the following drawing:

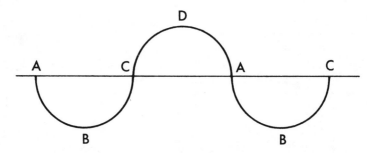

This emotional pattern is at work in the stock market, where it translates itself roughly as follows: Point A is the point at which large numbers of investors begin to realize that there is something wrong, both with the stocks they own and the stock market in general. They have just about given up hope that their stocks will go on to make new highs, and are now beginning to worry increasingly about whether they will be able to break even on their investment. It is even possible they are beginning to worry about how much they might possibly lose on their investments.

As prices decrease toward the ultimate bottom at point B, it becomes increasingly evident to more and more investors that something serious is wrong with the market. They gradually stop buying stocks and step up the tempo of their selling. Thus, their concern and fears become translated into a self-fulfilling prophecy. As more and more investors become anxious enough to act, they rush to sell stocks in greater numbers until, at point B, a psychological panic state occurs. Virtually everyone who is susceptible to the fear of losing money on his investment is finally panicked into selling, thereby alleviating the tensions brought about by his fear.

Once point B has passed, there is a period of calm, quiet, and generally low volume while people remember the intensity of the recent stock-market drop and maintain a posture of concern that a new decline will begin at any moment. Because everyone has already been frightened into selling, there is no more selling pressure on the market and, in fact, prices start to rise. Slowly, investors begin to regain their courage. At first, a few of the calmer or more sensitively tuned re-enter the market to buy stocks—then more and more in ever increasing numbers. During this phase the market begins to advance toward point C, or the point of so-called normalcy, where for a brief period of time stocks are selling for what fundamentalists believe they are actually worth.

By the time point C is reached, most investors have come to recognize that any chance of further decline has passed, and that a new bull market is again firmly established. They rush to take advantage of this state of affairs while there is still an opportunity for making money. They have heard of the success of the fortunate investors who purchased stocks near the beginning of the move, and have observed the large profits these people have already made. This success, and the increasing tempo of activity by others, excites and motivates them to imitate this same coup.

As more and more investors enter the market, it moves toward point D, where there is a mad, irrational urge to buy. Another climax—this time a buying climax—occurs and the tension caused by exhilaration is released from the minds of investors. After the investor has made his purchases, his emotional system is again brought into balance. He remains in a generally optimistic frame of mind, even though the stocks he bought may soon begin to settle slowly to a level below the prices he paid.

This doesn't concern him at first because he has seen that each brief drop in the market has been followed by a move on to new highs. He doesn't worry, that is, until the market again gets down to point A and he again realizes that something is wrong. He begins to worry once more and the stage is set for another round of unnecessary losses near the bottom.

The stock market thus becomes a rational phenomena when the investor comes to realize that he—and everyone else who operates in this market—are often irrational beings. Each person individually may be unpredictable, but taken as a group everyone's behavior can become predictable, provided it is possible to find a way to measure the group's irrationality.

The investor who knows this should be able to see that he can learn to be successful in the market, provided he can find some way to short-circuit at least that part of his emotional nature that leads him to his own peculiar forms of irrational behavior. Once he succeeds in this effort, the rest is easy. He is on his way to whipping the market.

7. Using the Cyclical Pattern

Once the investor has fixed in his mind the nature and the regularity of these cyclical tidal waves, he can learn to adjust his investment posture to harmonize with them. A simple series of rules for doing this follows:

1. Once the investor has isolated a clearly defined market bottom, and this can only be done in retrospect, he can be fairly confident that there

will not be another substantial market bottom for at least three or more likely four years. He may not know for certain that there will be a substantial bull market following on the heels of this bottom; it may be that the market will just drag along sideways, the way it did between 1946 and 1949, but at least he can be fairly confident that average stock prices will not fall drastically again for another few years.

This information may not seem like much, but when you are dealing with as may uncertainties and variables as there are in the stock market, this is extremely important intelligence. It alerts you to again become an aggressive buyer in the middle of a bear market, even though economic statistics and other news indicate that a further decline is likely.

2. If the market is in a period of panic with prices dropping very quickly, and if it is about 45 months or more since the last market bottom, you can be fairly confident of events. The termination of the decline will represent either the actual bottom, or be so close that you can anticipate the signals you will be getting a short time later and buy into the market decline.

3. Once the investor gets a buy signal within the context described in this book after a decline that is about four years past the period of the previous bottom, he can be sure that most of the investments he then makes will carry a low risk. They will be reasonably safe from any serious losses for anywhere from two to four years.

4. Any decline that begins much before three years after one of these clearly defined bottoms will usually be of short duration. Investors should not become excessively concerned about it, for usually it will be a better-than-average opportunity to buy stocks for the final flurry that usually comes at the end of every bull market.

5. If the market has been advancing for three years or more and the moving averages signal a coming decline, the investor should be more than normally concerned because the *time* for a general market decline is ripe.

6. General market declines normally last anywhere from 6 to 18 months. Very few persist beyond this period and these are usually interrupted by one or more rallies of at least six-months' duration that allow the investor to make attractive trading profits while waiting for the decline to end.

As you apply the specific techniques described in this book, it is always important to keep these six rules in mind as a general framework in which to operate. The investor will find that many times when the investment picture might otherwise be ambiguous, these general rules will help to clarify the picture.

PART III

Elements of a Coordinated Investment System

8. Objectives

We are now at the point where we can consider how to go about developing a coordinated investment procedure.

IN DEVELOPING ANY SORT OF METHODOLOGY, THE FIRST THING AN INVESTOR SHOULD DO IS DETERMINE SPECIFICALLY WHAT HIS INVESTMENT OBJECTIVES WILL BE AND THEN FIND SOME TECHNIQUE, OR A SERIES OF TECHNIQUES, THAT CAN BE UTILIZED TO ACCOMPLISH THESE OBJECTIVES.

Because most investors do not have precise means of signaling buy and sell points, their objectives change with the changing level of prices. If you yourself haven't done this many times, then surely you know someone who bought a stock for a trade and then, when it went down, converted his objective to "investing" until the stock went up to where he was "even with the stock" again.

It is important to realize the difference between the techniques used by a successful specialist and those of a trader. The specialist buys and sells stocks almost continuously to maintain an orderly market; the trader looks for stocks that offer the possibility of quick moves in the area of 10 to 20 percent over a period of 5 to 10 weeks. Both objectives require techniques different from those used by investors seeking to turn over their stocks approximately once each year. In turn all these techniques differ from the methods of pension funds designed to hold stocks for five years or more.

For example, the expense structure of the specialist is different from that of any other investor. In return for purchasing a seat on a stock exchange, a specialist pays no commission when he buys and sells stocks for himself. At the same time, he is supposed to make an orderly market in his stocks, which means that he is buying and selling stocks almost continuously throughout the day. It is not unusual for a specialist to buy and sell the same share of an actively traded stock two or three times every day. He considers a trading span of two weeks as long-term, and an average trading profit of less than $1/16$ point after expenses, a good rate of return on the money he has invested.

At the other extreme, a pension fund with assets of tens of millions of dollars must look for investments that will be reasonably safe and show a higher-than-average rate of return over a number of years. Because of their huge size, such funds are not able to trade in and out of stocks continuously the way a small investor can. If they become too aggressive, their market activities might tend to unduly influence—even break down—the markets. This in turn would be to their detriment. Therefore, they must learn to buy and sell stocks slowly over long periods of time, and they must be prepared at times to sit out the kind of bone-crushing bear markets that most other investors would not want to be a part of.

The pension fund looks specifically for many of the kinds of investments that you are told to avoid in this book. Often they look for defensive stocks to form an anchor for the rest of their investment portfolios, stocks that will not go down much in a bear market, even if this means these same stocks probably will not go up much during bull markets. They want stocks that pay better-than-average dividends with safety whereas we might not consider this the most important goal in our investment equation.

So each different kind of investor in the market has a different objective, and the way of achieving that objective varies in each individual case. If an investor wants to be successful, he must at some point clarify his objectives, and then be certain that the investment techniques he is using will further those objectives.

If you wanted to complicate the problem of obtaining optimum results, it would be necessary to apply different techniques: during bull markets, when the majority of stocks are going up; in bear markets, when they are going down; when the stock averages are indecisively churning around; for selling stocks short; and for buying stocks. An investor who deals in 100-share units does not require the techniques that one buying blocks in quantities of thousands or tens of thousands of shares needs.

To go into the differences and to expand on them would take a series of volumes, and this is not really necessary for the purpose at hand. What we have in mind for the present is something far simpler. It is a series of techniques that anyone with average intelligence and a willingness to work several hours a week at managing his own money can use to preserve his nest egg and make it grow under *all kinds* of market conditions. It is not necessarily the ideal system; techniques can be developed to work better under specific market conditions. But it is ideal in that it is the best compromise of all the factors involved that will work reasonably well under all market conditions. It also uses the least number of market statistics possible to obtain an overall view of the market. The objectives that our system, the Low-Risk Method of Successful Investing, is designed to meet are:

1. To help the investor select securities that offer the potential of a sustained price increase over a minimum of nine months, in order to take advantage of the more favored capital-gains treatment on profits held for nine months or more.
2. To allow the investor to remain invested in a stock for as far beyond this minimum period as it is profitable to do so.
3. To, at the same time, get an investor out of an ill-advised investment as quickly, and with as little loss, as possible when an error in judgment has been discovered (i.e., to limit losses of investment capital).
4. To adapt sound and relatively sophisticated principles to the needs of the average investor in such a way that anyone with no more than a knowledge of basic arithmetic can correctly and profitably use these techniques.
5. To be most useful to the small investor who purchases either odd lots or units of no more than 500 shares.
6. Except in a very broad sense, the techniques are not designed to anticipate either the exact tops or bottoms of markets, but rather are planned to show *when* a major change of direction has occurred *as soon after* the event as possible.
7. Most importantly, the techniques will show *when* to buy or sell, rather than *what* to buy or sell. Even the wrong stock purchased at the right time can be infinitely more profitable than the right stock purchased at the wrong time.

While the techniques in this book may seem unusually simple to those who are accustomed to more complex strategies, they are more than adequate for even the more experienced investors. Almost any investor who applied these techniques during the 1970 and 1974 bear markets would either have made money, or lost less money, on his investments in that market than with whatever system he was then using. Our Low-Risk Method is based on the idea that a little knowledge used to the fullest is much more effective than greater amounts of knowledge used haphazardly. *One of the greatest dangers in the stock market is knowing too much and overcomplicating the subject.* It is best to keep any investment program as simple as possible so that the investor can give himself ample time to review his investment strategy. Too many investors spend so much time maintaining their charts that they have no time to think about strategy.

These techniques require of an investor that he accept, for the time being at least, the premise that there are long-term trends operating in the market, that these trends cannot be manipulated but that they can be measured, and once measured, they can be utilized for profit. He will have to believe that these trends evolve into more-or-less repetitive cycles that result in two or three very sharp declines during the potential investment career of all investors, and that these declines result in what are virtually the buying opportunities of a generation. He should further be confident that the decline of 1973-74 provided investors with one of these rare buying opportunities.

He will have to accept the premise, too, that these techniques at the beginning and end of major bull markets will often signal him to take a course of action that may well conflict with what his friends, the newspapers, and perhaps even his own emotions tell him should be happening When this is the case, the investor should learn to operate on the basis of these techniques, rather than on the basis of his feelings. This may be very difficult to do initially, but in the long run, it will prove to be the most profitable course of action.

An investor will have to accept yet another premise. Once a trend is in motion it will continue in the direction of that motion for a sufficient length of time to prove itself profitable to follow. He will have to realize that the market casts shadows of its intentions so far enough in advance of the ultimate result that it will not be necessary for him to try to catch the exact tops or bottoms. Instead, he can work in harmony with the trend in motion at that particular time, knowing he has a technique that will give him a satisfactory portion of the potentially available profit in most of his investment attempts; he is at the same time protected from suffering large losses when he is wrong.

This really is all there is to good stock-market performance. An investor should invest conservatively; ride the tide as long and as far as it will take him when he is correct; cut his losses quickly when he is wrong; expect to be wrong occasionally; and avoid getting whipsawed too often.

9. How to Select Stocks

The techniques presented in this book will deal with *when* to buy any particular stock, rather than which stock offers the best relative value at any particular time. We decided upon this approach after observing for years that many stocks offering sound values languished in narrow trading ranges or went down, while numerous other seemingly over-priced stocks showed sizable percentage gains year after year. Our kind of approach cues the investor to the times when virtually all stocks should be avoided, and the times when almost any stock can be bought indiscriminately with fair assurance of capital gain—even though some stocks might hold more assurance of greater gain than others. The idea is to eliminate or minimize all possibilities of price shrinkage while you let those stocks that are appreciating in value grow at their own pace, regardless of value. This view is radically different from most other ways of approaching the market, and requires that many investors train themselves to both think of and act differently toward the market.

We arrive at the first obvious point of departure in our method of stock selection. When an investor uses a timing system, he has to eliminate from his investment patterns all thought of investing on tips, or recommendations from brokers or friends. He will have to condition himself to look at fundamentals differently. When he has money to invest, he will have to train himself not to ask, "What is the best investment to make at this time?" but instead, "Is this the right time to buy anything, or should I wait?" Most systems demand that the investor fragment his attention among large numbers of stocks at the time he is primed to act. They do not provide him with any real standard or constant to use as a yardstick against which to measure his alternative choices.

The techniques in this book differ in that they require an investor to select initially a small group of stocks, instead of trying to find the best stocks available at any particular time. Once he has made his selection, the investor will devote all his attention to these few stocks. Then, when the time comes to buy, he will make all his investment decisions from this limited group. Use of this method will require that the investor maintain certain weekly statistics on those stocks he preselects for possible purchase. As he maintains these statistics, he will acquire a greater awareness of the primary direction of both individual stocks and the stock market in general. Because all primary moves, both up and down, affect all stocks to at least some degree, the stocks in each investor's personal selection will provide more than adequate opportunities for profit, providing that the stocks are intelligently selected at the outset.

Once an investor determines what stocks he will watch, he must resist like the plague all recommendations, tips, and other enticements to invest in stocks outside of this group, because—as the investor should already be aware—such temptations usually turn out to be unprofitable distractions from the primary goal of making and keeping the top dollar from the market. If an investor finds that he cannot resist acting on a tip, he should do so only after he has subjected the tipped stock to the same standards he applies to the other stocks he follows. If the stock otherwise meets his requirements for purchase, he can then buy it. When this happens, the investor should add the stock to his selected list.

The statistics he maintains on his list of stocks are intended to tell him ideally when to both buy and sell every stock on the list. These are stocks that the investor has already determined in advance he would be willing to own. The statistics are designed to tell him this as near to the beginning of a move as possible, but in any event, not until after the move has already been *initiated* by someone else. The idea is not to try to force the market to do anything, but to benefit from what it already is in the process of doing.

It might seem unusual to select a group of investment candidates in advance, especially since you might possibly never invest in them. However, this is an adaptation of a principle used by the most consistently successful professionals in Wall Street, the specialists on the stock exchanges. Each stock-exchange specialist is assigned a small group of stocks in which he "specializes." Each of these men is in turn a member, or partner, of what is known as a specialist "unit," a group of from three to ten such specialists. These professional units handle only about 35 or 40 of the more than 1,000 stocks listed on the American Stock Exchange or the 1,500 stocks listed on the New York Stock Exchange. The stocks in which these men specialize are the only stocks most of them ever buy or sell. Nevertheless, because each man deals exclusively with only about six or seven stocks, he comes to understand their characteristics and idiosyncracies intimately. Under most market conditions, this knowledge enables him to make an excellent income, even though the number of stocks in which he invests is limited.

The fact that he or his partnership never invests in most stocks on the exchange where they are members does not prevent them from showing consistently profitable results. Dozens of other stocks not in their unit may be doing better than any of their stocks, but their own operations generally net them an adequate rate of return. It follows that, if this principle works well for the most knowledgeable and successful people on Wall Street, it ought to work equally well for the rest of us.

To summarize: CONCENTRATE YOUR ATTENTION. DON'T FOLLOW TOO MANY STOCKS.

The number of stocks an investor will be able to follow will depend on the amount of time he has available each week to spend on the market. For most people with full-time jobs, somewhere between 25 and 100 stocks will be more than adequate. With an inexpensive mechanical or electrical calculator costing as little as $10, it should take no more than two hours a week to maintain the necessary statistics on 100 stocks, as well as review these statistics every week to determine the proper investment strategy to follow. Any list with less than 25 stocks will probably not provide sufficient industry diversification from which to make meaningful selections.

The tendency of most investors, however, is to review too many stocks, rather than to follow too few. In its way, following too many stocks is just as bad as not following enough, because it confers on the investor the confusing prospect of having too many stocks from which to select when the important buying opportunities come along. It also takes too much time away from personal affairs, and sets up a condition whereby the investor spends so much time maintaining his records that he has no time left to digest their significance.

It is important to remember that retaining one's capital and making it grow once it has been acquired requires both skill and effort. Nothing grows without cultivation. Nevertheless, the effort to make capital grow, if intelligently applied, need not be as great as the effort that was expended to accumulate the capital in the first place.

To achieve a satisfactory rate of return from investing, however, an investor must allow himself the few hours needed each week to keep systematically abreast of the market. Nothing should interfere with this routine. When an investor skips a week from time to time and doubles up the following week, thus breaking up the regularity of the routine, it is like listening to a musical composition on a sound system that plays only intermittently. As a result, the investor fails to hear the total rhythm of the market and finds that his overall performance results deteriorate.

10. Preparing a Master Investment List

The first order of business is to decide how much time you as an investor are willing to spend each week on your investments. The amount of time is important because this is one of the two things that determine the maximum number of stocks an investor is able to regularly review.

The second determinate is whether or not the investor has access to a calculator to do the computations required in the Low-Risk Method. Depending on the speed with which an investor is able to perform his computations, one of the new electronic calculators should be able to do anywhere from five to twenty calculations for each computation he can perform manually.

Therefore it is again strongly recommended that an investor purchase a calculator as soon as he has convinced himself of the value of the Low-Risk investment concept. The time and effort he will save is well worth the small cost of calculators today. Competition in this area has in recent years brought the price down so dramatically that dozens of excellent calculators are available at very moderate prices.

For an investor who travels a lot, one of the so called "pocket calculators" might be suitable. These fit easily in vest pockets or brief cases and, best of all while traveling, they operate on rechargeable batteries.

An investor who has no need to take his computer with him might find a compact desk model a better bet. Desk calculators often have displays with bigger, more easily visible numerals. They also have keyboards which tend to have a more comfortable "feel" to them than the smaller vest pocket models. Consequently, not only are the small desk models easier to use but there is a tendency to make fewer errors when using them.

However, for the purposes of Low-Risk Investing, any of the inexpensive calculators on the market will more than suffice. They all perform the simple-arithmetic calculations accurately and much faster than you can perform them manually.

For a rough idea of the time required to maintain the Low-Risk investment statistics described in this book, use as a rule of thumb about two minutes per stock per week. It takes me about six to seven hours a week to keep tabs on a group of 300 stocks—less time when we're in the middle of a continuing trend, and more time when the trend is changing and major revisions to a portfolio are necessary. These two minutes per stock per week gives the investor the information he needs to know precisely the correct investment posture with respect to each stock on his master list.

An investor with only two hours a week to spend on his investments can easily maintain a list of up to 100 selection candidates. It is recommended that the investor limit himself to no more than 100 stocks. A list of 100 carefully selected stocks such as the model list we later offer provides the investor with a diversification that will be more than adequate to cope with any market condition.

It is important that the investor actually perform the calculations required to maintain a Master Investment List each week rather than turn the job over to a friend with access to a computer at the office. The reason is that in this way the investor gets "tuned in" to the flow of the market. This can be extremely important during uncertain market periods when contradictory signals are flashed.

11. Pick Only Stocks You Want to Own

Since the Low-Risk Method of successful investing works with a limited number of stocks from among the thousands of stocks on the market, the first order of business is to find some means of eliminating in wholesale quantities stocks that are not for any reason acceptable to you. Most of the following suggestions are offered for your guidance in doing so. When you have finished, you will have a master investment list of stocks that you will feel comfortable owning. From that point forward, your only concern will be to pinpoint first the right time and price to buy, then the right time and price to sell.

In this important respect, the Low-Risk Method differs from most other approaches. With the Low-Risk Method you continuously follow a small group of stocks you will sometime want to own. When a general market buying opportunity arrives or when you have money to invest, this continuous review simplifies the process of selecting the most attractive stocks of the moment. Conversely, if market conditions are poor, the method alerts you to hold off buying until market conditions are more favorable.

Most conventional approaches lack a continuing study of stocks. Instead, the investor with money to invest is likely to either go down a table of stocks until he finds something that "looks good," or buy a stock he overheard someone talking about at the club or at a party. Most "professional" counsel consists of nothing more than a broker naming upon request a good stock that the investor then accepts or rejects.

These purchases are usually made with little or no thought of timing them to take advantage of the broad swings in the market. When an investor is ready to buy, it is difficult to ask him to wait for a better time; he will either spend the money, or will no longer be in the mood to buy.

Because the master investment list is designed to contain only stocks the investor wants to own, it is important to consider his prejudices. Some investors will reject otherwise attractive stocks for various reasons, none of which have any bearing on the profit potential of the stock. Although this is to some degree irrational, it is nevertheless a fact that must be dealt with. Therefore, the investor who does not like to buy either very high or very low priced stocks; who is concerned with social issues, pollution, ecology, who is anti-liquor, tobacco, drugs, food additives, or whatever should exclude from his lists those stocks he associates with his biases.

Even if he disclaims his biases, he would probably find some reason for not buying, and the time he takes to review such stocks each week is wasted. It could much better be spent following stocks that do not evoke such strong feelings.

12. Don't Buy New Issues

Another broad limiting factor for most investors will be to ignore entirely all new issues. This suggestion is given with full knowledge that some of the most phenomenal price run-ups ever recorded have occurred in new issues during periods when the market for new issues was hot. It would seem, therefore, that new issues are logical candidates for investment consideration but this is not the case. *The object of low-risk investing is to both make and keep a good part of your stock-market profits.* History shows that very few people ever get to keep the profits from their new issues; many new issues fall apart during their first bear market and never recover because the company goes into bankruptcy.

This is true even of companies that seem to be of the highest quality. For example, around 1970 scores of Real Estate Investment Trusts came on the market. Most of these Trusts had impeccable pedigrees in that they were invariably sponsored by the nation's largest banks and insurance companies. The stock exchanges too were so enamored with these REITs that they made all sorts of exceptions to their rules to list these stocks immediately instead of first letting them season over the counter. Within five years these REITs turned out to be one of the biggest financial disasters in history. As a group the stocks dropped over 90 percent. In the process several dozen REITs were forced into bankruptcy.

If the new issue represents stock in a new venture that is just being organized, the mortality rate is exceptionally high. Most new companies do not have the right combination of intelligent, experienced management, adequate financing, and enough guaranteed backlog of business to succeed. Indeed, there are more people with the ambition and opportunity to start new businesses today than there are with the ability to nurse them to the point where they become profitably running enterprises. As a result, many new companies selling stock to the public are ill conceived, poorly financed, or otherwise unable to compete with larger, stronger, already established companies.

On the other hand, the new issues that represent strong, established, well-regarded, privately held companies going public for the first time are understandably brought out when demand for companies in their industry is strong. Consequently, according to our Low-Risk concept, the company is likely to be overpriced at the time of its issuance, even though it subsequently might sell higher.

The best time, therefore, to buy new issues is when they are no longer new issues. The best time to buy them is after their first market decline of consequence. During the decline, notice how well the company manages to survive. If its operations hold up or continue to grow, there will be ample time to buy at the end of the market decline. Often during such declines the stock will fall below its initial offering price. Thus, it becomes a better *and safer* bargain than it was originally. Even when it does not do so, the premium an investor pays is still worthwhile, considering the insurance he gets by waiting to be sure the company is viable enough to survive. While an investor might miss a big winner from time to time by following this rule, for the most part, he saves himself from investing in a string of stocks that will not survive. Always remember, IT IS PERFORMANCE COUPLED WITH SAFETY THAT BRINGS THE MOST WORTHWHILE RETURNS.

13. Don't Buy Most Over-the-Counter Stocks

This is not intended as a derogatory bias against the over-the-counter market. Many fine quality companies have always traded over the counter in preference to listing on an exchange and will continue to do so in the future. The admonition not to include over-the-counter issues in most stock lists is made because of the difficulty in the past of obtaining definitive trading statistics on O-T-C stocks. However, rapid changes in the structure of the markets are occurring daily and by the time you read this, this rule may no longer apply. What information can be had relates to quotation spreads rather than the actual prices at which the stocks trade.

The "spread" of a price quotation refers to the difference between the highest price a buyer is willing to bid or pay for a stock and the lowest price at which any seller is willing to offer his stock for sale at any given moment. In the O-T-C market, this spread at any particular time is usually (though not always) greater than that in similar quality stocks traded on exchanges. This makes an investor's cost of buying and selling O-T-C stocks higher, thereby lowering the eventual return on his investments. For this reason, unless an investor is absolutely certain he has a "sure thing," he should avoid the "counter." Nevertheless, if an investor is determined to include some O-T-C stocks in his list, he should be certain to restrict his selections to stocks that are regularly quoted in the newspaper he reads.

Similarly, with respect to stocks listed on stock exchanges, if the newspaper available to the investor does not carry the complete stock tables of all national and regional exchanges, he should restrict the stocks in his list to those whose prices are regularly reported in his newspaper.

14. Select Only Active Stocks

The best stocks to follow are those that are reasonably active. As a very rough guideline, avoid the stocks whose volume averages less than I,000 shares per day and that trade less than four out of five days each week.

There are, of course, many worthwhile stocks that trade less than this, but the 1,000-share average should be the guide for most investors. With at least this much activity, an investor can get into and out of a stock any time he wants or needs to without paying an exorbitant penalty when he first buys and then later sells the stock. Generally, the more active a stock, the "tighter" the market quoted on it.

For example, if an investor wanted to buy 100 shares of an actively traded stock at the market and if that stock last sold at $50, he could be reasonably sure of getting it for either 50⅛ or 50¼. On the other hand, if the stock was inactively traded, he might have to pay as high as 50½. Since the objective of investing should be to make money—and there are thousands of stocks to choose from, anyway—anything that will save the investor even $25 per trade should be included in his investment method.

15. Select Volatile or Cyclical Stocks

Most investment techniques shy away from volatile or cyclical stocks as too dangerous. Yet, properly harnessed, these so-called "dangerous" stocks offer lower risk and more certainty of profit than stocks generally thought to be safer.

The techniques in this book are predicated on the principle that the price of stocks is in continuous motion both up and down. Further, they are designed to capture not all, but a significant percentage of each movement. It therefore stands to reason then that the stocks an investor chooses to follow should be those that have shown in the past an ability to move both up and down more widely than is average. This increases the chances that they will continue to be wide swingers in the future. A stock that has not swung widely in the past will, in all probability, not move widely in the future. Furthermore, these narrower moves are more likely to be the kind that will unprofitably whipsaw an investor, and leave him with nothing to show for his time and efforts but small profits or a string of losses.

To determine the volatility of a stock an investor can use two techniques. First, he can ask his broker for a stock digest. The broker should be willing to give the investor a sample copy without charge. A stock digest is a monthly publication that provides many vital statistics about stocks in digest form, including price ranges, capitalization, earnings, dividends, etc.

To determine volatility, it is not necessary to concern yourself with all this data. You need only look at the price-range columns for the current and previous year, and then select stocks that have moved in a range of at least 100 percent between the high and low prices for both years. In other words, if the high of a stock was 60 and the low was 25, this issue would meet our criteria because the difference between 60 and 25 is 35 points, or 140 percent of 25. Because no investor can reasonably expect to buy or sell his stocks at their low and high prices respectively, he needs a price movement wide enough, after he adjusts for his margin of probable error, to make the effort worthwhile. Stocks that can move at least 100 percent above their low prices during most years offer the kind of probabilities for profit that make worthwhile the effort to capitalize on price movements.

Actually a 100 percent swing during the period of a year is not excessive, in light of a study made by a major brokerage house several years ago. This study concluded that—all things being equal—if there was no significant change in the operating outlook of an average company, an investor could expect to see the stock move about 30 percent above the low price during the year. If a stock moves in a 30-percent range when nothing is happening to either it or the market, it stands to reason then that there will be a much greater move in those stocks where something really significant is happening. By searching for stocks that have shown an ability to move widely, you are able to isolate in a fairly quick and simple manner those stocks in which the significant events are really happening.

The second, and preferred way to choose your list of stocks is to purchase a "chart book" that shows the weekly or monthly price ranges of a large number of stocks for a period of at least one full year. The longer the time period, the book shows, of course, the better it will be for your purposes. One excellent publication of this type includes a 12-year history of monthly price ranges for almost 1,000 stocks.

In the chart book, look for stocks that have a pattern of large, fairly well-defined moves lasting six months or more, with preferably 2 or 3 years of advancing prices and at least 6 to 12 months of declining prices. Look for stocks that under these circumstances double or triple in price from their lows each time they swing up.

A casebook example of this kind of stock is Needham Packing Corporation, which moved from 4½ in 1963 to 19 in February, 1965.

Observe in Figure 6 how the stock then dropped irregularly down to 3½ in 1966, turned around and again rose with force and power to 32 in 1968. The stock offered potential moves of over 300 percent to almost 800 percent on each swing, giving an investor significant room, even after allowing for a margin of error, to capture large amounts of profit. The stock began a downtrend in 1968 that continued through 1970. Under the rules described in this book, the stock registered a buy signal in January, 1971, at around $9. It began to move up shortly thereafter. If the past is any indication of what the future holds in store, it appears

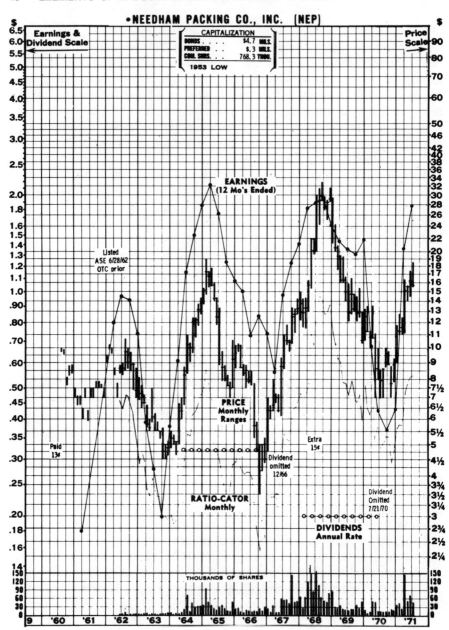

Figure 6 (Courtesy Securities Research Co.)

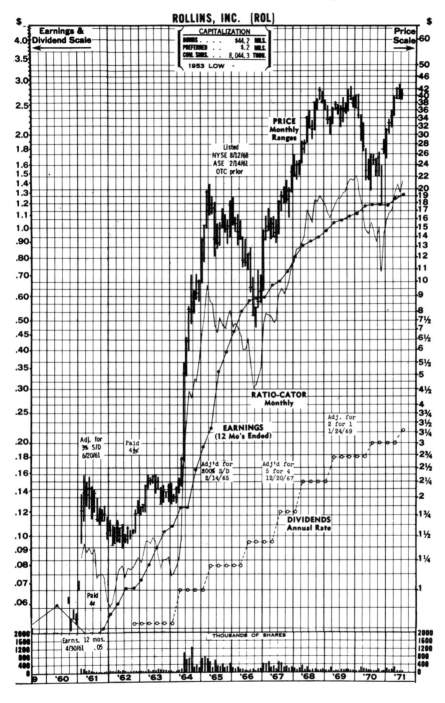

Figure 7   (Courtesy Securities Research Co.)

likely that Needham will again reward its bull-market investors with a substantial profit as the stock moves up to another bull-market top.

Stocks that fit the criteria for inclusion in a list of this type are generally the cyclical stocks, often ignored or not recommended by many analysts, and high-rate growth stocks, which often drop in price sharply during bear markets but which tend to retain investor interest. These stocks have the ability to resume their growth in a new bull market. An example of this is Rollins, Inc. (Figure 7), which went from 1⅞ to 20; dropped to 7¼, then moved up to 42 before dropping again to 22 during the 1970 bear market. The stock became eligible for purchase in November and December, 1970, in the $26 to $28 area and again in January, 1971, when it dropped down to $25.

A stock like this, provided it can maintain its growth momentum and

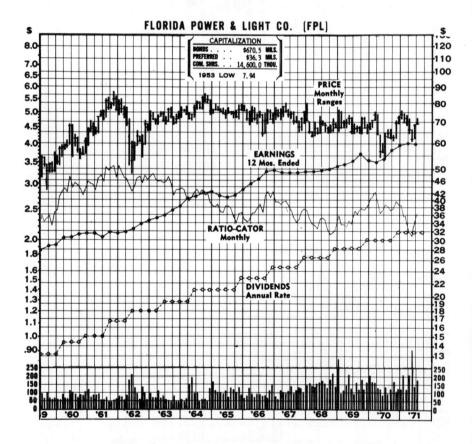

Figure 8   *(Courtesy Securities Research Co.)*

glamour image, often retains its following with an interested body of investors, willing to bid the stock up aggressively in price during bull markets.

On the other hand, the sort of stock an investor who desires to capitalize on wide price swings would tend to avoid is a stock such as Florida Power and Light Company (Figure 8), which was a satisfactory performer until 1962, but which for the next eight years was locked into a narrow range and rarely fluctuated much more than 20 percent per year.

The narrowness of these price movements does not permit sufficient opportunity for significant price appreciation during bull markets, and their advantage in bear markets is a negative advantage at best in that an investor owning a stock of this kind would suffer a smaller-than-average loss. However, since one of the objectives of these techniques is to be out of the market and in cash during price declines, the inclusion of such stocks in a portfolio is not necessary.

Again, this is not intended to be derogatory of F P & L which is an extremely stable, high-quality stock ideal for some investment programs though not ours. The programs for which it is best suited are those of large institutions that—because of their size or fiduciary requirements placed on them—are not in a position to turn over large amounts of stocks in a short period of time. The objectives of the portfolios outlined in this book, on the other hand, rely on substantial price movements, the ability to recognize major turning points, and the willingness to move in and out of stocks quickly when such action is required.

16. Diversify Among Industry Groups

Not only should an investor choose stocks that swing widely in price, but he should also attempt, insofar as it is practical, to have representative stocks on his list from as many different industry groups as possible. To determine industry grouping, he can obtain from the New York Stock Exchange their publication, *Common Stocks Listed on the New York Stock Exchange*. This booklet is free of charge.

In addition, *Barron's Magazine*, Standard and Poors, and others publish group indexes. It is possible to obtain a diversified stock list by choosing from the stocks in these industry averages.

The NYSE booklet identifies all the stocks listed on that exchange alphabetically and by industry group. This industry grouping makes the booklet valuable for use in conjunction with the chart book, because of the tendency of individual stock prices to move up and down in harmony with the overall market and also in sympathy with other stocks in their industry group. During each new bull market a few industry groups will out-perform the market. Virtually every stock in the group will move up in price much more than stocks in other groups. Then, too, each new bull market has its own super-stars. The groups that become the strongest performers of a new bull market are generally different from the industry groups that performed best during the previous bull market.

Therefore, in order to assure himself of some representation in whatever group is going to be the leader at any particular time, the investor should make an effort to diversify his interest among as many stocks as practical and select these stocks from as many different groups as possible.

In summary, the exchange booklet is useful because it segregates all listed stocks into industry groups. To obtain maximum industry diversification, therefore, the investor should include stocks in his list from as many different industry groups as possible. Just how many stocks from each group will depend on how big his list is. If he maintains a list of 50 stocks, then he should try to get one stock each from 50 different industries. This presupposes that he can find stocks in each industry that fit the standards for inclusion we have discussed in this book. If he maintains a list of 200 stocks, the investor should try to include one stock from each of the smallest groups, two stocks from the average industry groups, and no more than three or four stocks from the largest industries. This will provide him with more than adequate diversification to meet any market opportunity.

17. The Application of Fundamentals

After he follows the preceding suggestions aimed at eliminating from consideration vast groups of stocks, the investor will find that he still has a group of stocks much greater than he has decided he can conveniently maintain. For instance, he may have decided that 100 stocks are the right number of stocks for his Master Selection List, but after applying all the limiting factors we have discussed, he still has a list of almost 500 stocks to eventually narrow down to 100.

It is at this point that fundamental analysis comes into play. The investor should now take the 500 remaining stocks and segregate them into industry groupings. Initally he should see how many industry groups these 500 stocks represent and decide how many stocks from each industry he wants to include in his master list. Then he should use fundamentals to prune out the least attractive of these stocks in each industry one by one, until he is down to the number of stocks in each industry that he has decided to follow.

The use of fundamentals at this time can be as simple or as complex as the investor cares to make it. A simple, yet excellent, approach to eliminating stocks is through the use of the Standard and Poors Stock Reports found in most brokerage offices, or the reference sections of many public libraries. Each Stock Report contains on one sheet of paper a summary of the history, business, prospects, operations, and financial data of a particular company. It is suggested that these Stock Reports be reviewed in groups on an industry basis. If the investor has seven companies in the data-processing industry, for example, and he plans to include only two of these companies in his master list, he should plan to read the information on all seven companies in one sitting, on the watch for something to make him want to either definitely include or exclude each company from his list.

Because the investor has already culled the data-processing group down to seven companies, he presumably already has the most attractive companies in the industry on his list for low-risk investments. Therefore it should not really be a matter of overriding concern at this time that his fundamental review must be detailed. If he has the time and the inclination, the pruning process can be very detailed. Otherwise the investor can rely on a subjective or intuitive approach to more quickly prune his list down to the required two companies.

The two companies that finally remain should be the two in the data-processing group the investor would feel most comfortable owning in the event they ever flash "buy signals" at a time he has money to invest. This should be the primary consideration of his fundamental analysis, above all else.

Earlier in the book we appeared to minimize the value of fundamentals, not because of a belief that the analysis of basics is worthless, but out of a conviction that the way many investors used fundamentals did not really provide them with the kind of definitive yardsticks they needed. Instead of leading to conclusions relating to projected profitability of anticipated investments, most fundamental analysis does no more than provide facts that, while interesting, serve no more useful purpose than as conversational tidbits at cocktail parties. The reason for this is that fundamental analysis is designed to provide information relative to operating information such as financial profitability. Because the price of a stock is dependent only to a limited degree on corporate operations, and to a greater degree on investor attitudes toward these operations, most fundamental analysis is ill suited as a capital-gains, stock-selection tool.

It is the purported objective of fundamental analysis then, rather than the analysis itself, that is being challenged. In the investment equation, most fundamental analysis does not succeed in achieving its stated objective. As an investment tool, therefore, most fundamental analysis is worthless. Every investor who has studied the operating histories of companies probably knows dozens of examples similar to Florida Power and Light with superb fundamentals—companies whose operating revenues, earnings, and dividends have enjoyed uninterrupted growth for a decade or longer, while the price of the stock has remained on a virtual plateau. On the other hand, he is probably also aware of many other companies with highly erratic operations whose stocks regularly stage spectacular upside moves.

The investor thus senses that stock prices are not determined by precise, measurable, statistical values, but by expectations derived from constantly changing evaluations of:

1. What investors think will happen to a company in the future, based on whatever tools they have to work with.
2. What they think this will do to the price of the stock.
3. What actions they take to protect themselves by way of entering orders to buy, sell, or stand pat because of what they think will happen and how they expect everyone else to react as a result.

The investment equation becomes further complicated because each succeeding generation of investors insists on using different tools to measure what may happen to companies and for working out their investment actions. Thus, over the years, success has come at times to investors who participated in pool operations or who bought on the basis of dividend payouts, earnings payouts, cash flows, book values, sales growths, earnings growth, performance, concepts, limited floating supply of shares, etc., etc., ad infinitum. The approach that worked best at one time, however, may not even be moderately successful in the future. As for the more flamboyant methods, they may not even be legal.

It almost seems that just as a method becomes widely recognized and followed, something happens to make it lose its effectiveness. Throughout all these changing fashions of investing, however, there has been one certainty that could always be relied on. *Regardless of which investment approach is most successful at any particular period of time, the investor can rely on the fact that it will succeed in inflating the prices of those stocks favored by that strategy, dramatically and for an extended period of time.* Therefore, instead of tying himself down to an investment approach that may not be as successful in the future as it was in the past, or continuously changing investment approaches in a futile effort to be in step with the current fashion, the Low-Risk investor simply trains himself to recognize major price movements, regardless of their causes. He seeks to capture them as soon after they begin as possible. Once he becomes invested in a stock that is appreciating, he seeks to remain invested in that stock until the momentum of its price advance has been exhausted.

Accepting this as a premise for investing, then, an investor will not use fundamentals to determine which stocks to buy; only the price action of the stock will cue him to that. Instead, the investor will use fundamentals to choose those stocks he would feel comfortable owning, if and when their price pattern turned favorable.

A successful investor accepts the fact that a value, like almost everything else, means nothing until its time has come. Therefore, rather than trying to hold back the flood like the Dutch boy who stuck his finger in the dam, he will instead ride the tide like the surfer riding the crest of the wave. This may appear irrational at times, but he recognizes that it is the only rational approach to Low-Risk investing.

If the techniques an investor uses are sufficiently sensitive, he can operate with reasonable confidence and safety even on the final blow-off stages of highly speculative bull markets—markets, for example, during which stocks of marginal companies go from a few dollars to $25, $50, or more in less than a year.

The Low-Risk investment approach relies primarily on fundamentals during two periods of time: first, when initially setting up the Master Investment List; then, during one of the regularly occurring bear-market panic periods, when the investor should review his list with an eye toward replacing his weakest stocks with others more likely to outperform the market when the new bull market eventually arrives. Once an investor has made his selection, he should avoid changing his Master List during bull markets, unless some overriding reason seems to make a change in the list desirable.

Because bear markets are intervals that test the structural deficiencies of investors and companies alike, they are ideal times to determine how strong and adaptable a company really is. Almost any investor and almost any company can look good when overall conditions are favorable. A surprisingly large number of both groups, however, cannot stand extreme prosperity without becoming supercilious and insensitive. It takes a very adaptable, sensitive and level-headed individual or company management to negotiate through a bear market or other period of crisis. It takes people who correctly understand that bear-market crises are the spawning grounds of opportunity. Such people seek to capitalize on such periods, rather than permit themselves to be swept away by the hysteria of the moment.

Therefore, what an investor should look for during bear markets are companies on his list that are negotiating this period so poorly that they may either fold or fail to recover their former capabilities. He will want to replace these companies with others that are not only adapting well to adversity but perhaps are even growing as well. The use of intelligent fundamental research at such a time will re-structure his Basic List of stocks into an updated list of stocks that can out-perform or at least credibly perform relative to all others during the next bull market.

The elements to look for in such a review vary and no precise rules can be offered. For instance, a company may have stumbled early in a recession, but as the recession continues, the company gives evidence of having recovered and seems to be correcting whatever went wrong. Such ability to reconstruct its operations during a difficult period may well be a sign of extraordinary vitality. An investor might well decide to retain such a stock on his list on the theory that everyone makes mistakes, but the sign of true worth is the resiliency of being able to bounce back in difficult times. Therefore, a company whose management is adept enough to overcome its problems is likely to be a better company in the future than it was in the past.

On the other hand, if a company finds itself in serious trouble that the management has not anticipated—and worse, if it is incapable of adjusting to this difficulty—this tendency will become most evident during a recessionary period. Such a company should be eliminated from the Master Investment List.

There is one very important exception to this observation. Sometimes there are companies with enormous assets who, for some reason or another, get into so much trouble during recessions that their stocks fall in price to a point that reflects only a small percentage of their underlying assets. During the 1965-1970 bear market, three prime examples were Ling-Temco-Vought, which fell from 170 to 7⅛; Lockheed Aircraft, which plummeted from 70 to 7; and Penn Central, which dropped from about 86 to 5.

Similar disasters will occur in the future. At such times an investor will want to include at least a few such stocks in his shopping list. First, however, he must satisfy himself that any new management assigned to oversee the recovery of the company is reasonably competent and honest, and that any related reorganization will not eliminate the existing stock. When a company with such problems survives, its stock often offers possibilities not merely of large but of unbelievably huge capital gains.

As an example, a computation made a number of years ago showed that $l,000 invested in Chrysler at the 1932 stock-market bottom grew to

$27,000 in 1937, while both American Smelting and International Nickel appreciated to well over $20,000 during the same period of time. These three companies did not necessarily have the same problems in 1932 that confronted the Lings, Lockheeds, and Penn Centrals in 1970, but the same principle prevails—namely, *that a rebound from either a general panic or a panic centered in an individual stock can form the basis for enormous profits, providing that the company in question has the capacity to recover.*

To summarize, it is often possible to virtually ignore fundamentals entirely during bull markets. On the other hand, fundamentals are very important during bear markets to pinpoint the very weak companies that are not likely to survive the period of poor business that accompanies and sometimes follows bear markets, and the very strong companies that manage to grow and prosper during the bear market.

18. A Typical Master Investment List

After applying all the restrictive tests discussed on the preceding pages, an investor who wants to track a group of 100 different stocks might find himself with a Master Investment List similar to the following.

This list contains 100 stocks in 92 industry categories and sub-categories. With such widespread diversification in such a small list, the investor has more-than-adequate opportunity to profit from the swings in the market, regardless of the industries, price categories, or investment approaches that become fashionable at any particular time.

All the stocks in the group have enjoyed either continuous price growth or have been highly cyclical in the 1960's. All the companies appear to have survived both the 1970 and the 1974 bear markets intact. A few, such as Lockheed, might have been severely battered, but they nevertheless give sufficient evidence to the writer that they will come through this period if not stronger than ever before then at least intact. To others, the only visible effect was an interruption in their price, but not their earnings growth, thus giving an investor a chance to once more buy the stocks at attractive price levels.

The list contains both manufacturing companies and service companies. There are "story" companies, possible "turn-around" stocks, special situations, hidden-asset stocks, low-priced stocks, consumer-oriented stocks, investment-grade issues, and high-risk speculations; stocks with large floats and some with low floats, stocks well-known to investors and others of which he may never have heard, or of which he is only dimly aware.

On a list as diversified as this—regardless of where investor interest will focus in the future, regardless of which kinds of stocks will stage the most spectacular moves—at least a few of these stocks will always be among the market leaders.

The reader is cautioned, however, that this is a typical investment list. He is strongly urged not to use this list in its entirety as it appears in the book, but to modify it at least slightly to suit his personality and temperament. This admonition is made because of the perverse nature of the market and the manner in which it reacts to majority opinions.

If every reader of this book who decided upon a hundred-stock master list used these particular 100 stocks, it would lead to times when more investors would enter orders to buy or sell some of these stocks than the market can accommodate. The price mechanism would break down to the detriment of the investors. They would pay much more than they expected when buying and receive much less when selling. As a result, some of the anticipated profit from the investment is lost in the beginning.

Whenever too many investors decide to do the same thing at the same time, the market mechanism tends to break down. In the process it confounds the majority by acting contrary to their expectations.

Another advantage of custom tailoring a list is that an investor who picks stocks to match his individual personality pattern can buy stocks with greater assurance. Many successful investors often comment that they seem to have better luck with some stocks than with others. Personal experience has confirmed this observation.

TYPICAL MASTER INVESTMENT LIST

Industry	Stock
Aerospace	*Boeing Co.*
	Lockheed Aircraft Corp.
Aerospace Equipment	*United Technologies Corp.*
Air Freight	*Emery Air Freight Corp.*
Air Lines	*Braniff International Corp.*
	Trans World Airlines, Inc.
Apparel	*Hanes Corp.*
Atomic Energy	*United Nuclear*
Automobiles	*Chrysler Corp.*
Auto Parts	*Purolator, Inc.*
Beverages-Beer	*Schlitz (Jos) Brewing Co.*
Distillers	*Heublein, Inc.*
Soft Drinks	*Coca-Cola Bottling Co. (N.Y.), Inc.*

TYPICAL MASTER INVESTMENT LIST (Continued)

Industry	Stock
Broadcasting	CBS Inc., Co.
Building Materials	
Air Conditioning	Fedders Corp.
Cement	Texas Industries, Inc.
Heating	Crane Co.
Flooring	Armstrong Cork Co.
Chemical	Airco Inc.
	Dow Chemical Co.
Communications	Bunker-Ramo Corp.
Confectionery	Hershey Foods Corp.
Conglomerates	Gulf & Western Industries, Inc.
	Norton Simon, Inc.
Construction	Jim Walter Corp.
Containers—Glass	Anchor Hocking Corp.
Metal	Crown Cork & Seal Co., Inc.
Paper	Fiberboard Corp.
Copper	Anaconda Co.
Cosmetics	Avon Products, Inc.
Data Processing	Automatic Data Processing, Inc.
Drugs—Ethical	Marion Laboratories, Inc.
Proprietary	Bard (C.R.), Inc.
Drug Stores	Rite Aid Corp.
Electrical—Controls	Conrac Corp.
Equipment	Crouse-Hinds Co.
Household	Magic Chef, Inc.
Leaders	Westinghouse Electric Corp.
Electronics	Control Data Corp.
	National Semiconductor Corp.
Finance—Companies	Beneficial Corp.
Savings & Loan	Great Western Financial Corp.
Food—Bakers	American Bakeries Co.
Commercial	Gerber Products Co.
Dairy	Beatrice Foods Co.
Flour	Pillsbury Co.
Meat	Iowa Beef Processors, Inc.
Forest Products	Boise Cascade Corp.
Franchisers	McDonald's Corp.
Glass	Corning Glass Works

TYPICAL MASTER INVESTMENT LIST (Continued)

Industry	Stock
Gold	Campbell Red Lake Mines Ltd.
Holding Cos.	General Tire & Rubber Co.
	Natomas Co.
Home Furnishings	Kroehler Manufacturing Co.
Hotel Chains	Holiday Inns, Inc.
Insurance	US LIFE Corp.
Investment Trust	ASA, Ltd.
Iron Ore	Cleveland-Cliffs Iron Co.
Jewelry	Zale Corp.
Land	Louisiana Land & Exploration Co.
Lead, Zinc	Hecla Mining Co.
Leisure Time	Brunswick Corp.
Machine Tools	Warner & Swasey Co.
Machinery—Agriculture	Deere & Company
Construction	Caterpillar Tractor Co.
Industrial	Ingersoll-Rand Co.
Oil Well	Baker International Corp.
Steam	Combustion Engineering, Inc.
Maintenance	Rollins, Inc.
Metal Fabrication	Marathon Manufacturing Co.
	Norris Industries, Inc.
Metals—Miscellaneous	Engelhard Minerals & Chemicals Corp.
Mobile Homes	Fleetwood Enterprises, Inc.
Motion Pictures	Disney (Walt) Productions
Office Equipment	Addressograph-Multigraph Corp.
Offshore Drilling	Zapata Corp.
Oil—Crude	Kerr McGee Corp.
Domestic	Getty Oil Co.
International	Royal Dutch Petroleum Co.
Refinery	Quaker State Oil Refining Corp.
Optical	Bausch & Lomb Inc.
Packaging	Papercraft Corp.
Paper	Union Camp Corp.
Pollution Control	American Air Filter Co.
Photography	Bell & Howell Co.
Publishing	Dun & Bradstreet Co., Inc.
	Times-Mirror Co.

TYPICAL MASTER INVESTMENT LIST (Continued)

Industry	Stock
Radio-TV Mfg.	*Zenith Radio Corp.*
R.R. Equipment	*General Signal Corp.*
Real Estate	*Kaufman & Broad, Inc.*
Restaurants	*Howard Johnson Co.*
Retail—Dept.	*Marcor, Inc.*
Food	*Great Atlantic & Pacific Tea Co., Inc.*
	Supermarkets General Corp.
Mail Order	*Sears Roebuck & Co.*
Variety	*Kresge (S.S.) Co.*
Rubber	*Firestone Tire & Rubber Co.*
Steel	*Wheeling-Pittsburgh Steel Corp.*
Textiles	*Burlington Industries, Inc.*

PART IV

Computation of Moving Averages

19. Plotting Your Stocks

After deciding which stocks to include in his Master Investment List, the investor's next step is to assemble the statistical data necessary for knowing when to buy and sell.

The keystone of this Low-Risk Method is a mathematical tool known as the moving average. To arrive at clear-cut, unambiguous investment decisions with this method, it is necessary to compute moving averages relating to three different time periods for each and every stock. This sounds like a formidable undertaking and initially it is, but once the necessary moving averages have been constructed, the effort to maintain them takes only a few hours each week. Actually, the continuing weekly mathematics take just about one or two minutes per stock per week on an electronic calculating machine.

It is possible to purchase chart books with moving averages drawn on to the price patterns, but there are three principal differences between the Low-Risk method and these other, more conventional approaches. First, these moving averages are invariably computed for time periods different from those suggested for the Low-Risk Method. Secondly, most chart books draw in just one or two moving averages per stock, rarely three. A cornerstone of the Low-Risk Method is the correct use of three moving averages during different phases of a full market cycle. Finally, the Low-Risk moving averages give the precise price zones at which it is safe to buy or sell additional shares of stock after the initial signals at low or moderate risk.

To compute a moving average, it is first necessary to compute an initial average of the original number in the series under consideration. For instance, if we are working with five different numbers; 20, 21, 19, 18, and 22, their total is 100 and the initial average is 20. The average begins to "move" by starting with the current total (100), adding the closing price for the next week, subtracting the price of the most distant period included in the total, and dividing the new, updated total by the number of weeks in the average.

The following schedule will make this concept easier to understand. First, you have to post the closing price for the last five weeks. This is done in the column headed "Closing Price." The sum or total of these ices, or 100, is posted in the column "Five-Week Total." The s divided by the number of weeks in the average—in this case, -to get 20, which is the answer posted to the "Five-Week Average" column.

Week	Closing Price	Take-Away Price	Difference	Five-Week Total	Five-Week Average
1	20.0				
2	21.0				
3	19.0				
4	18.0				
5	22.0			100.0	20.0

This average begins to "move" at the end of the sixth week, when the closing price at the end of the sixth Friday, which we assume to be 23, is posted to the schedule. The price of six weeks ago is posted to the "Take-Away Price" column, and is subtracted from this week's closing price. Because this week's price of 23 is higher than the six-weeks-ago price of 20, the difference is a plus number of 3. If the closing price were lower than the oldest price, the difference would be a minus. The resulting difference thus obtained is either added to or subtracted from the preceding five-week total to get a new five-week total. In this case, the difference of +3 is added to 100 to arrive at a new total of 103. This new total is divided by 5 to get the new Five-Week Average of 20.6. After making the necessary postings, our schedule would look as follows:

Week	Closing Price	Take-Away Price	Difference	Five-Week Total	Five-Week Average
6	23.0	20.0	+3.0	103.0	20.6

If, during the following six weeks, the stock closed at 23, 22, 21, 24, 23, and 22 this is what the schedule would look like at the end of the period.

Week	Closing Price	Take-Away Price	Difference	Five-Week Total	Five-Week Average
7	23.0	21.0	+2.0	105.0	21.0
8	22.0	19.0	+3.0	108.0	21.6
9	21.0	18.0	+3.0	111.0	22.2
10	24.0	22.0	+2.0	113.0	22.6
11	23.0	23.0	—0—	113.0	22.6
12	22.0	23.0	−1.0	112.0	22.4

It can thus be seen that a moving average is a simple means of smoothing out fluctuating stock prices over a period of time. The longer the time period encompassed by a moving average, the smoother, straighter, and less sensitive is the moving average. The shorter the time period, the more sensitive and responsive to day-by-day fluctuations it becomes. To illustrate the difference in sensitivity of moving averages, the moving averages for three different time periods are shown on the chart of Trans World Airlines. Later on in the book, the use of these three moving averages in conjunction with other tools will be discussed to illustrate our timing methodology for buying and selling stocks.

The three time periods we will use are 5 weeks, 15 weeks, and 40 weeks. These periods were chosen because experimentation with numerous combinations has shown that these three time periods are best suited to produce the low-risk buy and sell signals used in connection with this system.

The signals produced using these three moving averages are designed to achieve the following objectives:

1. First, to keep the investor fully invested in any stock that has an extended bull market move, regardless of whether that move lasts six months or six years. Conversely, the signals are designed to keep an investor out of any stock during any extended period of declining prices.
2. To produce signals sensitive enough to indicate when a major change of direction has taken place at a point fairly close to the tops and bottoms of most major price movements.
3. At the same time, they are designed to be sufficiently insensitive to short-term market swings. This insensitivity eliminates many of the false signals or "whipsaws" that virtually all statistical and chart systems produce. These cause investors to buy a stock, then immediately sell it out at little or no profit a short time later.
4. To strictly limit the loss on the occasional bad investment that inevitably occurs, regardless of the investment approach followed.

What we have then is a system that simultaneously allows for open-ended, virtually unlimited profits at times and meanwhile strictly limits the loss potential.

These signals are further conceived to work reasonably well regardless of the pattern traced by a stock in its journey from top to bottom and back again. For instance, some stocks trace a sort of "V" formation whereby they rapidly plunge in value during a bear market, then quickly reverse themselves and move up in price just as fast as they had previously dropped. Other stocks form a sort of "W" bottom whereby they drop to their lows, then fail on their first attempt at a reversal. Such a stock will then fall back down to its previous low or perhaps drop slightly below it. Then, from this second low point or from its "double bottom," as it is called, the stock will turn around and begin what will become a strong bull-market move.

Other stocks trace out still different kinds of bottoms. Some look like ragged combs as a stock repeatedly falls into a stone wall-like area of support where people are waiting to buy. Some stocks never do form a visible bottom as such. Instead, they gradually slow down their rate of decline, then just as slowly turn around to begin an upmove. Such patterns tend to look like saucers. Many other kinds of bottoming patterns can be observed over a period of time, each of which is individualized by the specific circumstances of events surrounding the company and its stock at that particular time.

Contrariwise, at market tops, each of these bottoming patterns has a corresponding topping pattern. In place of a plunging "V" bottom, there is sometimes a soaring "A"-line peak. In place of a double "W" bottom, some stocks top out in a double-topped "M" pattern. And so it goes.

The challenge in developing a market technique both simple and effective was to find something that would work reasonably well under all possible variations. The three moving averages interpreted according to the rules set forth in this book fill the bill admirably, although obviously they will work better with some unfolding patterns than with others.

The 40-week moving average represents to us the life cycle of a stock during its own particular bull and bear markets. A stock is "born" into a bull market when its 40-week moving average turns up. It continues to grow as long as that moving average moves up. Then, when the moving average line flattens out and turns down, the peak has passed and the aging process, or the bear market in the stock, sets in. The degree of vigor in a stock is shown by the angle in which the moving average is tilted up from the horizontal.

While the 40-week average is advancing, the investment decisions most likely tó prove profitable are those based on bullish assumptions. Then, when the 40-week average turns down, a cautious or bearish investment strategy is likely to be most correct.

The 15-week moving average signals the seasons in a stock's bull-bear cycle. When the 15-week average first moves up above the 40-

week average, it marks the spring or the visible beginning of the stock's bull market. When it falls below the 40-week average, it marks the autumn or the visible beginning of its price deterioration.

The 5-week moving average smooths out the day-to-day prices of a stock, and often indicates when short-term changes of direction are going to occur within the context of the longer-term bull market.

A moving average, therefore, does three things. It smooths out all the price swings and jiggles for all time periods shorter than that of the average; it serves as a trend line of prices showing the direction in which prices are moving over the time period being measured; and it is, in effect, the line of normality above and below which the prices fluctuate.

The thing to realize here is that a moving average is not a horizontal line of normality but is usually tilted either up or down, depending on whether the primary direction of the stock is up or down. The law of trend lines is similar to the law of physics relative to motion; it assumes that a stock will continue to move in the direction of the moving-average trend line—whether that direction is up or down—until a force in opposition to it is first able to flatten it out and then change the direction of the line.

To illustrate how the moving averages of various time spans differ, let us examine the three different moving averages for the same stock. Our stock will be Trans World Airlines and the first moving average illustrated in Figure 9 is the 40-week average.

The line formed by computing the average price of the past 40 weeks is the least sensitive to change of all three time periods. Nevertheless, it portrays most accurately the primary direction in which the stock is traveling. This primary direction is the one that is usually of such long duration that it can be captured by investors for a significant amount of profit. This 40-week moving average is the cornerstone of all our work. This is the average that we speak of as casting a shadow of its intentions far into the future. When the 40-week line flattens out and turns up after moving down for six months or more, a stock is likely to move up for at least six months. When it flattens out and turns down, the next major direction in price is likely to be down. As a general statement, *all purchases of stock should be made only in harmony with this long-term trend;* that is, you should buy stocks only when this 40-week trend line turns up, and you should only hold your stocks as long as this line keeps trending up. You should not own a stock once this 40-week line has started to move down.

A close inspection will show that a moving average has a tendency to follow or lag behind the actual range of prices set by a stock. When a stock moves up for whatever reason, its price pattern will first rise above the moving-average line and then tend to lead or pull the moving average up behind it. On the other hand, when the long-term price patterns are down, as they were with most stocks during 1969 and 1970, the price pattern will fall below the moving average and tend to drag it down behind the falling price pattern.

One difficulty in the use of the moving-average technique develops when stocks settle for an extended period of time into a horizontal pattern, such as that charted by Florida Power & Light. When this happens, the moving average also becomes virtually horizontal. In a

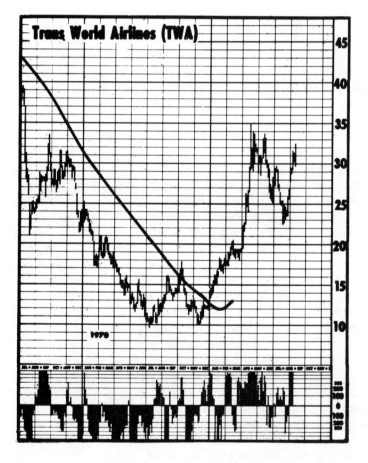

Figure 9   (Courtesy The Worden Tape Reading Studies)

stock such as this, the investor who follows orthodox rules for using the moving average as an investment tool and our own Low-Risk pattern of investing is likely to be whipsawed back and forth. He will suffer a continuous series of unprofitable trades as the operating rules indicate the stock should first be bought, then sold. This tendency to stagnate historically appears to occur more often with some stocks than others. That is why the investor was advised to pre-select for his list only those stocks with a tendency toward wide and regular price swings, rather than those that tend toward horizontal moves of limited amplitude.

Provided an investor had a chart of the price activity of Trans World Airlines back to 1969, a review of the movement of the 40-week average line would disclose that the moving average was slowly moving upward until early in April, 1969, at which time it reversed itself and turned down. Except for a brief period several weeks later, the moving average of TWA moved downward until January, 1971.

Following standard moving-average theory, an investor owning TWA and using a 40-week moving average would have sold his stock late in February, 1969, when the stock dropped below the moving-average price of 43. If he had the restraint, he would then have been out of the stock throughout the entire period covered by the chart coincidental with the bear market of 1969-70. Further, he would not have begun to actively consider the possibility of re-investing in TWA until the last week of September, 1970, when, for the first time in almost two years, the price of TWA moved above its moving-average price. However, since the moving average was still trending down at that time, the investor would have been uncertain as to whether this was really a new buy point. This uncertainty arises because the points at which stocks touch their long-term trend lines are just as often points from which a new move in the direction of a continuing trend begins, as they are early warnings of a change in the direction of the trend. The low-risk techniques that we will shortly explain will dispel this confusion, and will show the investor with precision just what he should have been doing at this point.

Nevertheless, although the investor still was uncertain at this point whether or not to re-enter the market in TWA, the use of the 40-week moving average by itself would have enabled him to sell his stock fairly close to the top, and would have kept him out of major trouble as the stock tumbled down to 10½ in May, 1970. While the use of the moving average may not permit the investor to re-purchase his TWA precisely at the low point for the stock, it will nevertheless enable him to do so at an attractive price, one that will probably allow him to make a worthwhile capital gain on his investment in the years ahead.

As one can see, the practical effect of selling TWA at around 43 and then coming back into the stock at these lower prices permitted the investor to make his money grow, even in a bear market. It allowed him to buy back more than 2½ times as many shares when the bear market was over than he would have owned had he held his stock all the way down during the bear market. This opportunity to buy greater numbers of shares for the same amount of investment capital during the periodic panic periods is the substance of which the pyramiding of wealth is composed. By taking advantage of these recurring opportuni-

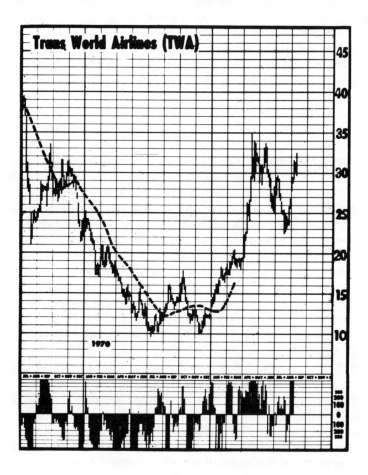

Figure 10   *(Courtesy The Worden Tape Reading Studies)*

ties, the investor is able to stay ahead of the inflationary forces at work that continuously dilute the value of the dollars he owns.

In addition, by not taking advantage of such opportunities when they occur, the investor places himself in the ever-present danger that he may have panicked as the stock tumbled toward 10½ and sold his shares at a loss. To compound his error, he might then have become too frightened to re-purchase the stock near the bottom as another cycle of price growth was about to begin.

The next moving average is the 15-week moving average designed to trace the intermediate trend of price moves. See Figure 10. Note that this average is more volatile than the 40-week average, but that it nevertheless follows the general direction of the 40-week average quite closely.

The 15-week line dropped below the 40-week average in April, 1969, just as the 40-week average recorded its highest weekly posting. In falling below the 40-week line, the 15-week average confirmed that investors should have sold their TWA five or six weeks previously at 43. Once the 15-week average dropped below the 40-week line, it remained there for the duration of the decline. On February 4, 1971, the move of the 15-week line above the 40-week line suggested with a high degree of probability that the bear market in TWA was over, and that the stock was again established in a new bull-market uptrend.

Finally there is the 5-week moving average. A review of the chart in Figure 11 will show that it is the most volatile of all. The trend line of this average changed direction sixteen times, and crossed the 15-week average eight times during the bear-market decline.

After the investor has selected his stocks according to the guidelines suggested, he must next construct 5-, 15-, and 40-week moving averages for all the stocks on his list. Once this is completed, the next step in the Low-Risk investment system is to update these moving averages each week. The price data he will need to do this can be obtained either from back copies of financial newspapers in a library or by posting the closing prices from a stock chart. Obviously, posting from a chart will result in numerous small fractional errors because it is difficult to determine precisely closing prices. It is difficult when posting from a chart, for instance, to know if a closing price is 42½ or 42⅝. These errors should net themselves out, however, and are a small price to pay in return for the time saved in preparing a master list this way.

Once the Master Investment List is set up, the investor need not maintain charts on his stocks, or post his moving average figures onto any kind of graph. It is only necessary that he keep his figures updated on a schedule similar to that shown to the right.

Because so many additional columns are needed to maintain three separate moving averages on one schedule, the "Take-Away Price" columns of our earlier example are modified. The investor will no longer post a price in these columns each week, for the columns have been eliminated. Instead the investor merely checks off the price he is subtracting in the appropriate column 5, 15, or 40 weeks back. The "Difference" column has also been eliminated; the difference between the current price and the take-away price is posted directly to bring the moving average up to date, as shown on the following schedule:

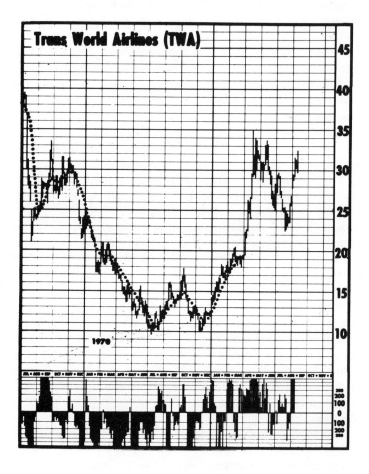

Figure 11   (Courtesy The Worden Tape Reading Studies)

LOW-RISK METHOD DATA-POSTING SHEET (TRANS WORLD AIRLINES)

Date 1971	Price	Take-Away Price 5 Wk	15 Wk	40 Wk	5-Week Total	5-Week Average	15-Week Total	15-Week Average	40-Week Total	40-Week Average	
1-8	14⅜	X			64⅞	$12.97	193⅞	$12.91	526⅝	$13.16	
15	15⅞	X			68⅝	13.72	192	12.80	526¼	13.15	BUY
22	16½	X			73	14.60	192⅝	12.84	527⅝	13.19	
29	18	X			78½	15.70	196¾	13.12	531⅞	13.29	
2-5	16⅞				81⅝	16.32	201¼	13.42	533¾	13.34	BUY
11	18				85¼	17.05	207½	13.83	537¼	13.43	
19	17¾				87⅛	17.42	212¾	14.18	541½	13.54	
26	18⅛				88¾	17.75	219⅜	14.62	547⅝	13.69	
3-5	20⅜				91⅛	18.22	228⅞	15.25	555⅝	13.89	

Standard moving-average theory recognizes four basic rules with respect to moving averages. These are illustrated on the following charts, whose publisher used a weighted 30-week moving average (the solid line) and a weighted ten-week average (the dotted line). We will be paying particular attention to the 30-week line, and all comments contained herein will be made with respect to that line.

1. When the trend line is moving upward, every time the price of a stock approaches, or temporarily penetrates the trend line, the stock can be purchased.

   Under these rules, Roosevelt Raceway was eligible for purchase at $26, $28, $34 and $40 according to the chart in Figure 12.
2. When the trend line turns up after having been in a downtrend, a stock should be purchased when its price penetrates the moving average and remains above it for several weeks.

   A textbook example of this is Milgo Electronics (see Figure 13), which penetrated its moving average and became qualified under these rules for purchase at about $16.
3. When the trend line is moving down, every time the price of a stock approaches or temporarily penetrates the trend line, the stock should be sold or sold short.

   The price pattern of Condec (Figure 14) illustrates this rule.
4. When the trend line turns down after having been in an uptrend, a stock should be sold when its price penetrates the moving average and remains below it for several weeks.

The price pattern of Compudyne (Figure 15) illustrates this rule.

The use of moving averages in the Low-Risk method differs from the standard use of moving averages in one important respect. In the Low-Risk approach, the relationship of one moving average to another determines the basic investment posture at any particular time. According to standard moving-average theory, the relationship of price to the moving average determines basic investment posture.

With the Low-Risk approach, the periods of uncertainty so common to other approaches are eliminated, along with many of the whipsaws, because action is deferred from the time the stock itself first rises above or below its 40-week moving average. It does not occur until price movement has been sufficiently sustained to drag with it its shorter-term averages above or below the trend line.

Experience shows that when a stock has been in a long-term downtrend, its ability to move above its 40-week line and stay there long enough for its 5-week average to register higher than the 40-week average, is sufficient evidence to assume that its downtrend has been reversed. Conversely, after a stock has been in an uptrend for an extended period of time, the drop of its average price over a 15-week

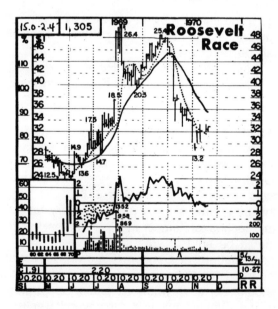

Figure 12   (Courtesy R. W. Mansfield Co.)

period below this 40-week price is sufficient evidence that the momemtum of its upward drive has been dissipated.

20. What Is the Market Doing?

An investor must assemble two additional items after he has selected a master list of stocks and prepared the moving-average statistics necessary to making investment decisions.

The first of two essentials for a coordinated investment program involves the use of a recognized market-wide stock-price index such as the "Dow Jones Industrial Average," the "New York Stock Exchange Composite Index," or the "Standard and Poors 500 Stock Index." There is a lot of controversy among statisticians as to which of these or other indexes is best to use, but for our purposes it really doesn't matter. The "Dow Jones Industrial Average" is the oldest, best-known, and most widely circulated so it is the one most investors may prefer to use. Also, it is the one most likely to be available in local newspapers.

I prefer to use the "New York Stock Exchange Composite Index,"

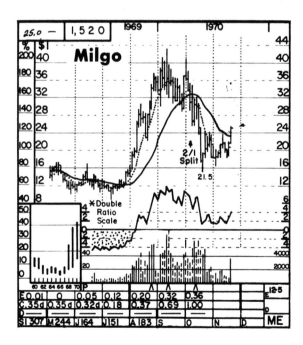

Figure 13   (Courtesy R. W. Mansfield Co.)

primarily because it is composed of all the common stocks listed on the New York Stock Exchange while the DJI contains only 30 of the top "blue chips" on that exchange. Surprisingly, however, for the manner in which the price index will be used in this program, approximately the same results will be recorded at approximately the same time—regardless of which index is used. For illustrative purposes, this text will use the DJI because of its greater accessibility.

Once the investor decides on his index, it is necessary for him to construct on a weekly basis the same 5-, 15-, and 40-week moving averages that are maintained for each stock. These averages, like the individual stock averages, are based on the closing value of the index each Friday (or on the last trading day of the week if it is ever anything other than Friday).

21. What Are Most Stocks Doing?

Finally, it is necessary to know what the majority of stocks are doing. It would appear at first glance that this question is the same as the previous one; and that an investor has the answer to this when he

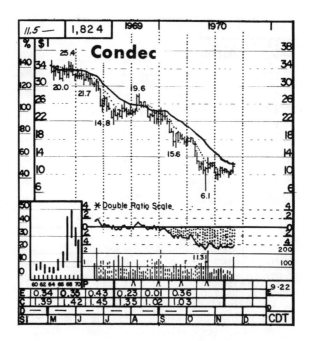

Figure 14   (Courtesy R. W. Mansfield Co.)

posts the weekly movement of the Dow Jones market average. But eventually the investor will come to realize that, at certain especially critical times, the average price of stocks will be going in one direction but fewer and fewer stocks will be traveling in that direction.

Very often, especially after the market has been going up for a considerable period of time, there is a tendency for prices, as measured by a price index, to continue to move up while, slowly but steadily, the trends of more and more stocks will reach their individual price peaks and start to move down. The reason the indexes appear to hold up well is that, during the final phases of a bull market, those stocks that have been the speculative favorites of the bull market will be staging outstanding performances as they move on to their final bull-market highs. It will not be unusual to see such stocks move up in price as much as two to ten points per day, and, of course, each move disproportionately affects a price index. At the same time, and under the cover of these spectacular moves, more and more stocks will be closing each day either unchanged or moving down imperceptibly, perhaps an eighth or a quarter point a day.

Eventually, this almost imperceptible resistance to further advance

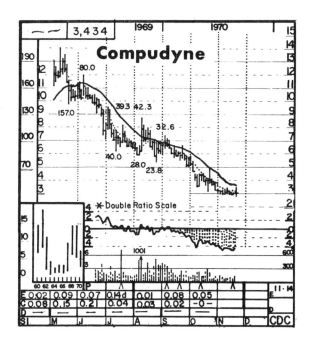

Figure 15   *(Courtesy R. W. Mansfield Co.)*

will drag down the price index, but it does not do so immediately because of the upward pull of the star performers. As a result, the market gives an appearance of being healthy when actually the opposite situation is the case.

In order to compensate for this phenomenon, it is necessary to construct another group of moving averages. These averages consist of the net differences between the *number* of stocks closing higher and the number of stocks closing lower on the New York Stock Exchange. Experience has shown that neither the 5- nor the 40-week Advance-Decline average is of sufficient benefit for the average investor. It is therefore suggested that only the 15-week Advance-Decline moving average be posted weekly.

After he has worked with Advance-Decline statistics for awhile, the investor will discover that often they have a tendency to turn down shortly before the price index at market tops. Likewise they are often slow to turn up once an uptrend has been established.

This tendency becomes especially valuable for a conservative yet performance-oriented investor because it alerts him to become especially cautious whenever the A-D, as it is called, turns down. With this early warning signal, he learns not to expose his portfolio to undue market risk at such vulnerable periods in the market. Conversely, knowing that the A-D is slow in turning up is a valuable tool in hand for confirming the existence of the market advance that was signaled earlier by the Dow Jones average.

To construct a 15-week Advance-Decline line, it is necessary to start with an arbitrary number such as 20,000, or any other number an investor chooses. Then refer to the financial pages of a Sunday newspaper or any other publication that carries a summary of stock-market activity for the week. The statistical section of the paper will contain a table showing the total number of stocks that advanced and the number that declined during the past week. Subtract the number of declining stocks from the number that advanced, then add or subtract this difference to the arbitrary number with which you started.

For instance, let us say that during the current week 1766 stocks traded; 1061 advanced, 520 declined, and the rest were unchanged. Subtract 520 from 1061:

$$
\begin{array}{rl}
1061 & \text{advances} \\
-\ 520 & \text{declines} \\
\hline
+\ 541 & \text{(net advances for the week)}
\end{array}
$$

We find that 541 more stocks advanced than declined. We take this plus 541 and add it to our arbitrary base number, which for the sake of this illustration is 20,000, to get a cumulative A-D number of 20,541.

If in the following week 710 stocks advanced while 832 stocks declined, we see that:

$$710 \text{ advances}$$
$$\underline{-832 \text{ declines}}$$
$$-122 \text{ (net declines for the week)}$$

A total of 122 more stocks have declined. When we return to our cumulative base figure of 20,541, we should subtract 122 to get a new cumulative A-D number of 20,419. We do this for 15 successive weeks then add together the cumulative A-D totals for the past fifteen weeks in the same manner that the closing prices for stocks were totalled. This figure is divided by 15 to get the current week's moving-average value for the Advance-Decline line.

There is a practical reason for starting off with an arbitrary number such as 20,000. This index often deals with negative numbers and many people get confused working with negative numbers. It is possible to eliminate this difficulty by starting off with a plus number so large that the investor need never worry that his accumulated total will end up as a minus.

Nevertheless, if for some reason during an especially severe decline the A-D line does fall into minus territory, it is possible to adjust for this by simply adding another arbitrary 10,000 to each of the cumulative figures of the past 15 weeks. This step will make each of the past 15 moving average totals greater by 10,000, but will not otherwise change or confuse any calculations; the usefulness of an Advance-Decline line is not in how high or low the numbers go, but in the direction they are traveling at any particular time.

To get an idea of how subtle the Advance-Decline line is, and at the same time how important it is at market tops, look at the charts in Figures 16 and 17.

First, study the Down Jones average in January, 1966, at point #1. Notice how the Dow approached 1,000, backed off, and then very briefly moved above 1,000. At the same time the A-D line did not go on to a new high when the Dow moved above 1,000, but was in fact lower than it had been at the time of the previous rise to the 1,000 level. This was a sign that there was trouble in the market. Here an investor may have suspected that the advance was running out of steam and a decline was about to start.

Another example of this type of action was noted at point #2 in 1967. The Dow approached 930, backed off, then went on to 950. On the move to 950, the A-D line again did not go on to a new high but just reached the level it had achieved earlier when the Dow was at 930.

At point #3, the A-D line was already beginning to turn down, while

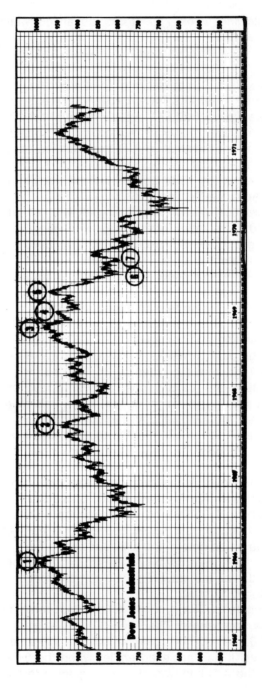

Figure 16 (Courtesy The Worden Tape Reading Studies)

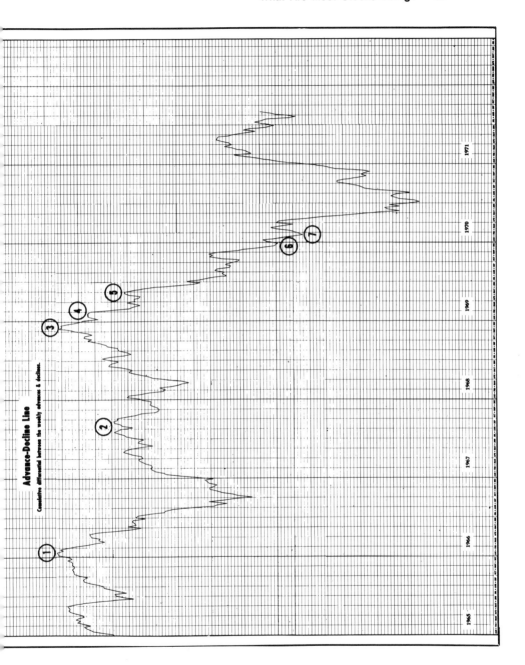

Figure 17 *(Courtesy The Worden Tape Reading Studies)*

the Dow was going on to a new high, again hinting that the advance was coming to an end.

ADVANCE-DECLINE LINE

Date 1970	Adv.	Dec.	Diff.	Cumulative Diff.	15 Week Cum. Diff. Total	15 Week C.D.T. Average
Jan 3	1,100	481	619	17,784	287,266	19,151
9	918	711	207	17,991	285,585	19,039
16	474	1,168	(694)	17,297	283,625	18,908
23	566	1,018	(452)	16,845	281,271	18,751
30	196	1,416	(1,220)	15,625	276,569	18,438
Feb 6	931	669	262	15,887	271,425	18,095
13	875	700	175	16,062	266,608	17,774
20	992	617	375	16,437	261,930	17,462
27	1,166	417	749	17,186	258,650	17,243
Mar 6	976	654	322	17,508	256,837	17,122
13	465	1,153	(688)	16,820	254,699	16,980
20	506	1,101	(595)	16,225	253,039	16,869
27	1,278	326	952	17,177	252,997	16,866
Apr 3	725	861	(136)	17,041	252,990	16,866
10	439	1,163	(724)	16,317	252,142	16,809
17	257	1,384	(1,127)	15,190	249,548	16,636
24	199	1,446	(1,247)	13,943	245,500	16,367
May 1	439	1,189	(750)	13,193	241,396	16,093
8	383	1,231	(848)	12,345	236,896	15,793
15	250	1,400	(1,150)	11,195	232,466	15,498
22	154	1,523	(1,369)	9,826	226,405	15,094
29	1,175	494	681	10,507	220,850	14,723
Jun 5	918	699	219	10,726	215,139	14,343
12	328	1,273	(945)	9,781	207,734	13,849
19	1,093	484	609	10,390	200,616	13,374
26	221	1,415	(1,194)	9,196	192,992	12,866
Jul 2	455	1,092	(637)	8,559	185,326	12,355
10	998	624	374	8,933	177,142	11,809
17	1,246	359	887	9,820	169,921	11,328
24	935	664	271	10,091	163,695	10,913
31	914	663	251	10,342	158,847	10,590
Aug 7	599	966	(367)	9,975	154,879	10,325
14	401	1,176	(775)	9,200	150,886	10,059
21	1,228	384	844	10,044	148,585	9,906
28	1,442	233	1,209	11,253	148,643	9,910 Buy
Sep 4	1,155	463	692	11,945	150,726	10,048
11	873	710	163	12,108	152,363	10,157
18	953	665	288	12,396	154,033	10,269
25	1,128	518	610	13,006	157,258	10,484

Figure 18

At point #5 the A-D was much lower than at point #4 even though the DJI was higher. This indicated that the bear market was not yet over; it had much further to go.

Although the Dow at #7 was higher than at #6, again the advance decline line was lower, implying that still-lower prices were in the wind.

If the interpretation of these signals appears too illusive for you to handle at this time, do not be overly concerned. This is just another example of why chart reading is more of an art than a science. This is also why our moving-average techniques were developed—so that you could know precisely what action to take and when to take it.

For instance, Figure 18 is a sample of an Advance-Decline line in midsummer, 1970, that shows you just when it turned up to give the first indication that it was again safe to begin buying stocks. The signal came on August 28, 1970, when the Dow was at 765.81. We shall learn how to make practical use of this information shortly.

These are the only tools an investor needs to achieve reasonably good investment results. Many analysts suggest the use of any number of additional "indicators," but this puts too great a burden on an investor, and does not allow him sufficient time to study the implications of his calculations. *A thorough knowledge of a few simple tools is generally more valuable than a superficial knowledge of many.*

There is one final comment to make before we proceed to a discussion of how these tools interrelate into a composite stock-market program for profit. If most of the stocks in an investor's master list are listed on the New York Stock Exchange, the NYSE Advance-Decline statistics should be maintained. On the other hand, if the majority of stocks on his list are listed on the American Stock Exchange, then the Amex Advance-Decline statistics should be maintained. These two series of statistics parallel each other, but from time to time they do give different readings. To be in tune with the particular group of stocks wherein most of your investments will be centered, you will be wise to use the Advance-Decline statistics most closely related.

PART V

How to
Profit from
the Market

22. The Analytical Tools

The investor is now at the point where he has prepared the necessary schedules for all the stocks on his master list. He is now ready to make investment decisions based on these schedules.

To review, the following moving averages are being maintained on a regular weekly basis:

1. For each of the 50 to 200 stocks in your investment universe:
   a. 40-week moving average.
   b. 15-week moving average.
   c. 5-week moving average.
2. The Dow Jones Industrial Average:
   a. 40-week moving average.
   b. 15-week moving average.
   c. 5-week moving average.
3. New York Stock Exchange
   weekly summary of advancing and declining stocks:
   a. 15-week moving average.

23. How to Time the Primary Trend

THE UP PHASE   To determine his primary investment posture at any given time, the investor need only be aware of what is happening to the Dow Jones Industrial index and the cumulative Advance-Decline line.

In order to know when to begin to buy stocks, let us first assume that we are now in a bear market and that both the 15-week A-D line and the 40-week Dow Jones moving average are declining. Here is what you do:

1. FIRST AND FOREMOST, DO NOT BUY ANY STOCKS AT ALL WHILE BOTH THESE AVERAGES ARE DECLINING. When both averages are dropping, the primary trend of the market is down, and the odds against your finding one of the few stocks that may successfully manage to swim against this tide are too high to make the risk worthwhile.

This is the most important piece of advice in this book. If you remember nothing more than this rule *and have the discipline to follow it,* you will earn your return from the purchase of this book.

2. Wait until *either* the A-D line turns up or the 5-week average moves above the 40-week average. It is at this point that your investment program to buy stocks should begin. Generally, the A-D line will be the tool that gives you your first buy signal. It will usually precede the moving-average signal by two to four weeks.

3. As long as the A-D line keeps advancing or the 5-week average remains above the 40-week average, it is safe to keep adding to your portfolio, using the formula we will discuss shortly.

4. If either the A-D line or the 5-week moving average turns down before you reach step #5, stop buying any more stocks but do *not* sell the stocks you have already purchased unless the rules for selling individual stocks tell you to do so.

5. The first purchases an investor makes near the end of the bear market have to be treated as trades and not as investments *until* the 15-week DJI average line manages to move *above the 40-week average. When the 15-week average moves above the 40-week average, an investor can be reasonably sure that he is in a bull market that will last for at least six months and possibly much, much longer.*

6. By the time step #5 is reached, you should be fully invested to the limit of your resources. You should then remain fully invested until you get a signal to begin converting your stocks into cash.

It is important at this point to note that speculation in the stock market is an art and not a precise science. You should therefore clearly understand that the rules we have just read, and those which will follow, do not guarantee that you will never lose money or that you will always make money on your investments. Successful speculation involves the ability to balance certain fixed working procedures with a knowledge of the probabilities. Certain events usually, though not always, follow in a sequence that can be anticipated. The Low-Risk Method, although it always gives precise rather than ambiguous signals, does not guarantee that a stock will never go lower after you buy or higher after you sell.

What the signals give is a reading or an indication of the probabilities.

What does a "buy" signal after a substantial price decline signify? What you are actually getting is an indication that the risk of *further* substantial price erosion is small, while the probability is favorable that the stock will either move sideways for awhile or advance in price from current levels.

On the other hand, a "sell" signal after an advance warns you that *the risk of holding the stock much longer is high*. There now exists a good probability that the stock will either move along sideways or drop in price from current levels.

No one knows exactly what is going to happen tomorrow. Nevertheless, while it is not possible to know precisely what will happen, with practice an investor can train himself to measure future probabilities. By so doing, he can learn to anticipate the future with a high degree of certainty because very little in the universe happens at random.

Generally there is an inter-relationship between what happened yesterday, what is happening today, and what will happen tomorrow. Events always cast their shadows in respect to the future direction of prices. Nevertheless, the future is at the same time in a state of continuous modification and revision. The amount of modification is factored into the techniques we are describing through our means of using shorter-term moving averages in conjunction with the 40-week average.

To observe how a bull-market signal evolves, look at the following charts (Figures 19 and 21) of the Dow Jones Industrial index as that index came off its bear-market bottom in 1966.

These charts show a 13-week and a 39-week moving average. The Securities Research Corp., when preparing this chart, uses a 13-week calendar quarter as its basic unit of time. This time period works well for the averages, but I encountered some difficulty in applying it to individual stocks; the results were not nearly as consistent as with use of the 5-, 15-, and 40-week time periods suggested. Nevertheless, for the averages, these charts give results that are similar to those you will get with your 15-week and 40-week averages. The market hit a low of approximately 740 during the second week of October, 1966, then began its recovery. The 15-week A-D line turned up during the second week of December, the first signal that it was all right to again buy stocks. The Dow at this time was 820. Signal number two came during the last week of January when the Dow was at 860. This occurred when the 5-week DJI moved above the 40-week line.

Finally, the 13-week average crossed above the 39-week line during the third week of February, 1967, confirming the probable existence of a new bull market. At the time it happens, we have to say "probable" because no one can be absolutely sure about anything in the stock market. Nevertheless, periods during which profitable purchases of stocks could have been made have occurred consistently after this point, making this signal as reliable as anything you can get concerning the market.

From the third week of February on, an investor should have been *fully* invested for as long as the 13-week or his own 15-week average remained above the 40-week line. This ability of prices to rise so that their average price for 15 weeks remains above their average price for 40 weeks indicates that the overall emotional interest of investors is directed toward buying, rather than selling stocks on balance. Therefore, the momentum of the market is in the direction of continuously rising prices. The investor should remain fully invested for as long as this condition exists.

Figure 20 is another example of how the bull market signal of 1970 developed.

First, as we have previously observed, the Advance-Decline line turned up during the week of August 28. That week, the DJI closed at 765.81. This was the initial signal to begin a program of reaccumulation after the long 1968-1970 bear market.

Two weeks later, on September 11—with the Dow slightly off at 761.84—the signal to step up the tempo of purchases occurred when the 5-week short-term moving average crossed the 40-week average on the up side.

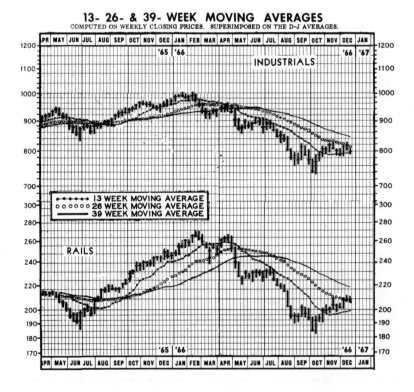

13- 26- & 39- WEEK MOVING AVERAGES
COMPUTED ON WEEKLY CLOSING PRICES. SUPERIMPOSED ON THE D-J AVERAGES.

Figure 19   (Courtesy Securities Research Corp.)

The third, and confirming signal, of the birth of a new bull market came during the final week of September, according to the 13-39 week chart in Figure 20, with the Dow at 761.77; and on October 16 when the Dow was 763.35, according to our 15-40 week formula. No matter which week an investor used as the birth of a new bull market, the difference was negligible inasmuch as the Dow subsequently moved much, much higher. This rise assured the investor a handsome profit on almost any stock he purchased between August 28 and October 16, 1970, according to our rules.

THE PHASE OF INDECISION   As a bull market travels on its road to maturity, it has a tendency to pause from time to time. At these times it is sometimes difficult to determine in advance whether the bull market is going to end prematurely, or whether the pause is merely a period

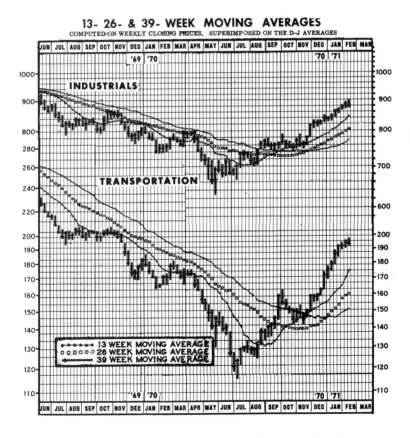

Figure 20 (Courtesy Securities Research Corp.)

during which the market re-gathers strength for another move to new higher price levels. If the market is merely resting, then an investor will want to remain fully invested, but if the pause is the prelude to a downturn, he will obviously want to sell his stocks out as close to their tops as possible. As a result, even though an investor may be aware of the probabilities at any particular time, he does not know precisely what the market is going to do next.

To resolve this indecision, the following strategy permits the investor to remain fully invested as long as it is safe to do so, and at the same time alerts him to the possibility of having to quickly sell all his stocks.

Whenever the 15-week moving average of the Advance-Decline line turns down, or either the 5- or 15-week price index drops below an advancing 40-week average (as it did late in 1967), one should change his investment strategy. All new purchases of stocks shoud be deferred for the time being as though in fact a new bear market were beginning. In other words, don't buy any more stock until the picture clarifies because the risk created by the uncertainty is too high to make additional new purchases worthwhile (see Figure 21).

The deferral of new purchases until the picture becomes clearer, however, does *not* mean it is necessary to sell any or all of the stocks already in your portfolio. *The sale of any stock, once it is purchased, is not predicated by what the overall market does from that point forward. Instead, the sale of any stock becomes predicated by its own market behavior in conjunction with overall market conditions.* Although most stocks do have a tendency to be affected by the overall trend—especially during the final phases of both bull and bear markets—each stock tops or bottoms out at its own particular time, based on its own peculiar combination of fundamentals, political, and emotional factors. This may be in advance of or later than the action of the overall averages.

If the overall market trend is in a phase of indecision, as it was in early 1968, an investor may well go through this period with most of his portfolio intact. If, however, the decline turns into a full-fledged bear market, one should soon be largely in cash by selling one after another of his stocks as they top out. The investor will then be waiting—patiently, it is hoped—with cash in hand to take advantage of the bargains that will be available at the birth of the next bull market.

The December, 1967 drop of the 15-week average below the 40-week average turned out to be temporary, a mere pause in the advance. The Dow Jones index subsequently went on to approximately 1,000. But the thing to remember is that while this was the expectancy at the time, it was not a certainty. Therefore, the decision to be cautious when the 15-week index dropped below the 40-week index was then (and always is) the correct decision to make.

THE DOWN PHASE   Ultimately, there will come a time when the 15-week A-D line turns down, as it did early in 1969, and the 15-week price average drops below the 40-week average, representing not merely a period of hesitation but a full-fledged bear market. Since this investment concept is extremely conservative, the same investment strategy applies during a bear market as during a period of hesitation: Namely, the procedure is to defer all new purchases of securities until the primary trend shows promise of becoming favorable again. In the meantime, investments should be sold whenever their trends indicate that their individual tops have been seen.

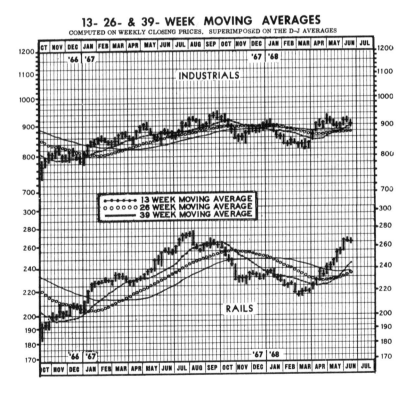

Figure 21 *(Courtesy Securities Research Corp.)*

24. How to Time the Purchase of Individual Stocks when the Primary Trend is Down

There is just one strategy to follow when the primary trend is down. The strategy, as we have already indicated, is to *wait for the market to turn up before buying anything*.

Fortunately, bear markets do not last forever and, if you are patient, you will be rewarded with a golden opportunity to buy at bargain prices. Near the end of each bear market there comes a time when the market begins to grope for a bottom and build a base from which it can start to advance again. When this appears to be happening, the investor should once again begin to consider the purchase of stocks for his portfolio. A review of the activity of the market after the 1966 decline revealed that the Dow industrial average made a low at 740 and moved up 110 points to 850 before the primary bull market was confirmed by our rules. A new bull market is confirmed when the 15-week DJI price line rises above the 40-week price line. This was the safest point at which to become fully invested, but this point of confirmation did not come until four months after the low point of the market, a time when much of the cream had already been skimmed off the beginning of the new bull market.

There is a correlation in the stock market between risk and return. Ideally, the correlation is that the more the risk, the greater should be the reward; while the more certain your prospects, the less you should expect in the way of a return. On Wall Street, things don't work this way, however. On Wall Street, by the time most investors become fully invested in stocks, not only is the cream gone but so is most of the milk. About all that is left is a bottle of chalky water. By the time the average investor becomes confident of buying, the risk of loss to him is so high that in many instances it is a virtual certainty that he will lose money.

On the other hand, when the majority of investors are thoroughly frightened by what they assume to be a high degree of risk, the actual risk of investing is often so low that the potential rewards to investors are almost beyond belief.

What we will try to do here is to zero in on these times when the risk of making an initial investment for each individual stock is the lowest. We will begin by assuming that we are in a bear market. As the bear market has progressed, we have sold one after another of our stocks so that we now are sitting with cash that we are looking to invest when the time is right. The bottom of a bear market is, of course, the best time to invest because at the bottom an investor can often get from two to ten times as much stock for each dollar of investment as he can get at a market top.

However, there is no way to know exactly when the bottom of a bear market has occurred, nor is it possible to know exactly which stocks will be the next bull-market leaders. *But the probable leaders of at least the next rally in the bear market, if not the next bull market itself, are most likely to be those stocks that moved up in price during the most recent decline, or those that went down the least and recovered the fastest.* In either case, these are the stocks that have the confidence of aggressive investors. Accordingly, they are stocks that the average investor will want to own as soon after the market makes its turn as possible.

During a bear market, two conditions confront the investor:

1. The 15-week Dow Jones moving average is dropping lower and is also lower in price than the 40-week moving average.
2. The 15-week moving average Advance-Decline line is moving lower.

While this set of conditions persist, the investor should shift his focus and pay particularly close attention to the behavior of the 5-week price index and the 15-week Advance-Decline index. If he is normally conservative, he will not begin to buy stocks until the 15-week A-D line turns around and begins to move up. He will get a confirmation of the wisdom of his action when the 5-week D.J.I. moving average moves above the 40-week D.J.I. average.

But if our investor is a more nervous and aggressive type, then he can fine tune the bottom of a bear market even more precisely and come in a lot closer to the final bottom of the market. The price of this fine tuning, however, is a higher degree of risk, because he will probably be wrong several times along the way toward the final bottom. Therefore, he should understand that in all probability he will from time to time during the progress of the bear market wind up trading rather than investing; and he will almost certainly have to accept a few more small trading losses along the way in favor of this greater opportunity.

If he is able to adjust to this greater degree of risk in return for a chance at a bigger profit, he should proceed as follows. As soon as the 5-week Dow Jones industrial moving-average index moves upward, the investor has a good indication that the market trend has turned, or is about to turn and go up for at least the next several weeks or months. The investor does not know at the time if the market at this point has made its ultimate bear-market low. He must realize that this may be just one of those periodic rallies that characterize a bear market. There is no way to know this with certainty until some date in the future after the ultimate market low has been thoroughly tested and visibly established in retrospect. However, by the time the investor can be certain of a new bull market, investor psychology will have become noticeably more optimistic and the prices he will have to pay for the best stocks will be much higher.

Therefore, while the investor does not know then whether or not the market has made its ultimate low, he knows that any time the 5-week average turns up, the market has reached a point from which at least a significant rally is likely to occur. When this happens, the investor should scrutinize his list of stocks for those with the 15-week average above the 40-week line even by as little as one cent. They are the strongest stocks in the investor's universe in that they have demonstrated their resistance to decline during that most recent phase of the bear market. It is this ability to resist the general declining tendencies currently in effect that designates them as the stocks to purchase. When the selling pressure is lifted, they will be the stocks with the greatest built-in power to lead the advance. As the advance continues, more and more stocks will fall into this category. Be on the alert for them and include them in your investment portfolio until such time as you become fully invested.

An example of a stock with superb resistant tendencies during the summer of 1974 was United Technologies. In December, 1973, although the Dow still had one year and 250 points to go until it touched its bear market bottom, UTX already made its bear market low at 21. From that point on it began a slow steady advance in contrast to the poor market action of most other stocks. By the time the Dow touched bottom in December, 1974, UTX was already well on the way toward doubling in price during the next six months. (See Figures 25 and 26).

As early as the first week of June, 1974, the 15-week moving average at $27.24 rose above the 40-week price at $27.11. These two moving averages are not only valuable in that they indicate the direction of probable price movement, but they also indicate to an investor the price range at which purchases should be made. The rule to follow is to make all purchases of stock at prices that are within or below the level of the three moving averages.

On June 7, 1974, the 40-week average price of United Technologies was $27.11; the 15-week average, $27.24; and the 5-week price, $27.23. The price at which the stock should have been purchased was somewhere between $27.11 and $27.23 and indeed the stock did close that Friday at $27⅛ permitting a purchase within our Ideal Buying Range.

The Low Risk investment rules caution us not to buy any stocks during bear markets except on those occasions when the 5-week Dow Average turns up. This action gives the first hint that the market is attempting to gather sufficient strength to stage a substantial rally. A purchase made on this date enabled a very brash and aggressive investor to buy UTX at a price that was to prove to be very near the bottom. Subsequently the stock traded in a range between $24 and $28 for about four months before it began its climb to $79.

A review of the UTX chart shows that it was indeed possible to buy the stock on a number of occasions in the Ideal Buying Range. On October 18, the 5-week Dow Average turned up once more; then down the following week, and up once more, this time to stay, in November. At these times the stock traded mostly in the $28-$29 range. Note how close to the bottom it was possible to buy these stocks at prime times of fairly low risk by using the simple rules outlined in this book.

Note how much stronger United Technologies was than the Dow during this entire bear market period. This is typical of a stock that often outperforms the general market for whatever reason when a new bull market begins.

BROCKWAY GLASS   Another example of the opportunity to find good investments with relative safety at major turnarounds is Brockway Glass as evidenced in Figure 24.

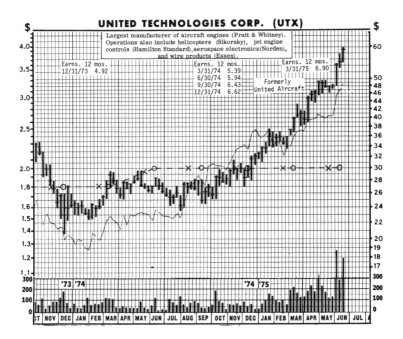

Figure 22

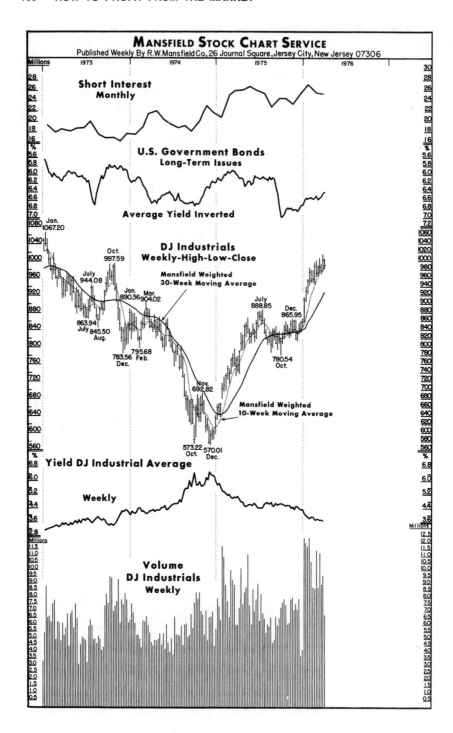

Figure 23

On October 4, 1974, when the Dow closed the week at 584.56, Brockway was still in its downtrend. Its closing price was $10¼ and its moving averages were: 5-week, $10.53; 15-week, $10.92; 40-week, $11.76. Then quickly it began to consolidate and reverse its trends. Four weeks later, on November 1, the 5-week average at $11.23 moved above the 15-week average at $11.20. Another two weeks later, on November 15, the 5-week average, now $12.03 rose above the 40-week average at $11.77. When the 5-week average moved above the 40-week average in this manner, the stock became a candidate for purchase in the event the general market flashed a buy signal.

That signal came on January 10, 1975 when the 15-week Advance-Decline line turned up for the first time since April 5 of the previous year. By January 10 Brockway's 15-week average was above its 40-week average. Consequently, if this stock was in an investor's Master Investment List, it would have been considered as a purchase candidate on January 10 at $13½.

Almost immediately the stock moved into the $14½-$16½ area. While it was not possible to buy the stock in an Ideal Buying Range, the stock was nevertheless a worthwhile purchase because after resting in the $14½-$16½ range for about two months, the stock embarked on a sustained advance which took it to $36 by mid-1976.

Figure 24 (Courtesy Securities Research Corp.)

25. Timing the Birth of a New Bull Market

The birth of a bull market cannot be timed with any certainty before it begins. It is possible to anticipate approximately when a new bull market should begin by keeping in mind the longer-term cyclical possibilities discussed earlier. That is, we know that in recent years significant market bottoms have occurred about four years apart, which is just another way of saying that bull markets are born about every four years.

But you cannot tell in advance which specific day will mark the birth of a new bull market. You only can anticipate it in general terms. For instance, cyclical expectations were for the 1968-1970 bear market to end sometime between August, 1970, and February, 1971, and for the new bull market to develop at that time. Instead, however, the bull market was born prematurely in May, 1970 when the Dow hit a bear-market low of 627.46, and was confirmed in retrospect as an accomplished fact during the August-February time period. Then, in 1974 the expectations were for the bear market to end some time between May and October. But just as in 1970 the bear market ended three months earlier than anticipated, in 1974 it lasted two months longer than expected.

A bull market can be verified only after the fact and usually after the market is much higher. By this time, a substantial part of the big, safe, early profits of a new bull market already have been missed by most investors. Therefore, it is necessary to tune ourselves more finely into the beginning of a new bull market in the manner we have just illustrated. To anticipate the possibilities of a new bull market, we need to observe the following:

1. At some point in the bear market, the 5-week DJI moving average will turn up. This will signal either a strong rally in a continuing bear market or the first rally in what later on will be recognized as a new bull market.

   If it is a rally in a bear market, it is often of sufficient amplitude to trade profitably. If it is the first rally in a new bull market, it will be the point at which those stocks that will lead the new bull market will first begin to assert themselves. The new bull-market leaders are available now at bargain-basement levels for the last time in the bull market.

   An aggressive investor willing to trade will now buy stocks, knowing that he might have to sell them out a few weeks or months later, possibly at a small loss if the move turns out to be nothing more than a bear-market rally. He knows also that he will be extremely well positioned for the start of a new bull market, if that is what will come out of the rally.

A more conservative investor will do nothing at this time but wait and meanwhile put the finishing touches on his shopping list of stocks for the next bull market.

2. If, during the rally, the 5-week moving average shows sufficient strength to rise above the 40-week DJI line, the conservative investor is alerted to the possibility that this is more than just another bear-market rally. He should then immediately start to buy a few of the strongest stocks, in anticipation of a forthcoming confirmation of a bull-market signal. While he is buying his stocks at this point, the investor is aware of and accepts the possibility of some further risk in the market until the bull market is fully confirmed.

3. Another indication of a forthcoming bull market is given when the 15-week A-D line stops declining and first turns up.

4. Under our system, a bull market is finally confirmed when the 15-week DJI line rises above the 40-week line. At this point all signals are GO. The investor should rush to become fully invested if he has not already done so, and he should remain fully invested until he gets his next bear-market signal.

5. Once a stock is purchased under any of the preceding circum-stances, it is not to be sold on the basis of any general market signals. The general market sell signal is designed only to tell the investor to avoid making new purchases for the time being. Once a stock has been purchased, however, the action of the stock itself will determine how long it should be held.

It is possible that a stock purchased as a trade during a bear-market rally will be held for several years if the stock tells you it is sufficiently strong to retain. On the other hand, something unforeseen might happen to a stock bought as an investment near the beginning of a bull market that will cause you to sell it out several weeks later.

To summarize then, a movement of the 15-week DJI average line above the 40-week line signals the existence of a new bull market that was conceived several months earlier in the final panic stages of the previous bear market.

26. How to Time the Purchase of Individual Stocks when the Primary Trend is Up

As the primary trend moves up, very little should be done with most portfolios. The investor should wait patiently until the bull market has run its course, then step in to sell his stocks, one by one, and reap his harvest of profits.

However, *because all stocks have a tendency to top out individually in successive waves,* one or more stocks in any particular portfolio may mature and be ready for harvest at a time when the overall market still has enough momentum left to move higher. There will also be times when an investor will have accumulated some extra money to invest, and will not wish to wait until the end of the next bear market to invest these additional funds. Under these conditions, the safest rules to follow are these:

1. As long as the 15-week DJI average continues to travel above the 40-week average, and
2. As long as the 15-week Advance-Decline average continues to move in an uptrend,

additional purchases of stocks can be considered—provided that the choices are taken from among the stocks in your list that meet the following tests:

1. Ideally, the stock should be one that is making, or has just completed, a late bottoming formation. The 5-week average price of the stock has just moved above the 40-week price, and the 15-week line is moving up rapidly toward the 40-week line.
2. Alternately, look for stocks that have previously given buy signals and are now reacting to the point where their prices are down to the ideal buying point in the area between their 15- and 40-week average prices. In this category, look for stocks selling as close to the 40-week price as possible to limit the amount of risk.
3. An initial purchase of a stock can be made when the short-term line first crosses the 40-week line. After this point, however, always wait for stocks to get down to the ideal buying range before purchasing. If the market is so strong that the investor can find no stocks in this category, and he feels he must make a purchase, then the best thing he can do is to refrain. With some personality types, it will be difficult to wait for a point of safety, but if such an individual ever hopes to achieve consistent success, he must at some point in his investment career acquire the necessary patience to wait until he is fully invested and then wait to sell at the proper time.

IN SUMMARY, NEVER MAKE A NEW INITIAL COMMITMENT IN A BULL MARKET UNTIL THE 5-WEEK AVERAGE RISES ABOVE THE 40-WEEK AVERAGE. IF YOU DON'T BUY AT

THIS TIME WAIT FOR THE PRICE OF THE STOCK TO DROP DOWN TO THE "IDEAL BUYING RANGE."

The following is an example of each category of buy signal. Assume that the averages have already signaled the existence of a bull market and we still have some money to invest. Admiral Corp. is the kind of stock that made a late turnaround. It was not until the week of October 2, 1970, that the 5-week average of the stock first moved above the 40-week line. That week the chart appeared as in Figure 25.

The averages were as follows:

Closing price	$9.37
5-week average price	8.99
15-week average price	7.85
40-week average price	8.75

With this signal, Admiral became a purchase candidate. The first purchase would have been made immediately at approximately 9⅜. The ideal purchase range for the stock as of October 2 was between $7.85 and $8.75; and the secondary purchase range, between $8.75 and $9.00. Whenever the stock dropped into either range, preferably the lower one,

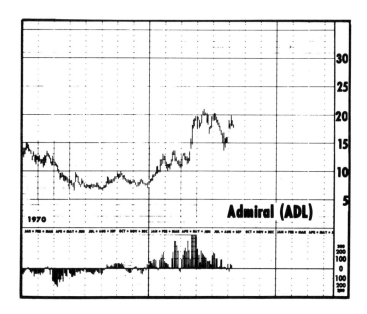

Figure 25   (Courtesy The Worden Tape Reading Studies)

it became a candidate for additional purchases at very low risk. Then, as long as the 5-week price held above the 40-week price long enough for the 15-week average to rise above the 40-week price as well, the stock should have been held. If during this time the 5-week average again dropped below the 40-week line before the 15-week average gave its buy signal, the stock should have immediately been traded out of the portfolio.

Movement of the 15-week line above the 40-week average is considered confirmation of that stock's bull market. The issue is safe holding as long as the 15-week average remains above the 40-week average.

The stock dropped into the Low-Risk buy range during the week that ended October 16. At this point it was feasible to make additional purchases of Admiral. The stock did not move up in price immediately

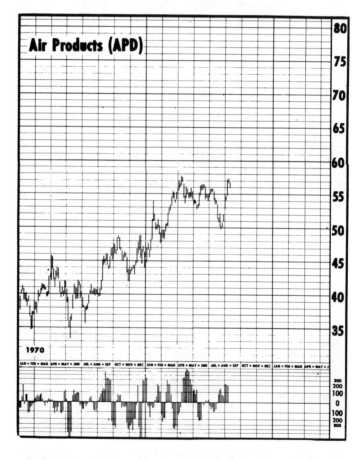

Figure 26 *(Courtesy The Worden Tape Reading Studies)*

but instead drifted down to a low of $7.00 over the next ten weeks before starting to move up again.

On November 6, 1970, three weeks after drifting into this Low-Risk range, the 15-week average moved above the 40-week price, confirming the existence of Admiral's bull market, and—as we can see by the chart—very shortly thereafter the stock began strong advance in price.

Our second example, in Figure 26, illustrates how a subsequent re-purchase area is determined.

Air Products Corp. was one of the leaders coming out of the 1970 bear market. As the chart shows, its bear-market low was made back in October, 1969. As the stock moved up quickly from the May, 1970, lows, it hit some profit-taking resistance during the week of November 6. On this date, as the stock sold off from a high of 48⅝, its statistics were as follows:

Closing price	$42.37
5-week average	45.80
15-week average	44.50
40-week average	41.67

This closing price of $42.37 briefly put the stock into the Low-Risk purchase zone between $41.67 and $44.50. The stock was available for purchase on the following Monday at prices ranging between $42.00 and $42.50, then very quickly ran up to $54.00 before reacting again. A purchase in this Low-Risk zone very quickly proved profitable.

27. How to Time the Sale of Individual Stocks when the Primary Trend Is Up

Once a stock has been purchased, an investor's primary emphasis should shift from concern as to what the general market is doing to what the particular stock or stocks in his portfolio are doing, although he should at the same time remain aware of the overall market trend.

During a primary bull market, a stock should be retained in a portfolio as long as its 15-week price remains higher than the 40-week average price. When the 15-week average drops below the 40-week average, the stock should be sold, not immediately, but as soon as the stock rises back up into its ideal selling range.

The ideal selling range in this case becomes the reverse of the ideal buying range at a market bottom. At a market top, the ideal selling range is the range of prices between the 15-week average, which is now below the 40-week price, and the 40-week price. The secondary selling range is the range between the 5- and 15-week prices.

A DROP OF THE 15-WEEK PRICE BELOW THE 40-WEEK PRICE TELLS YOU THAT THE RISK OF CONTINUING TO HOLD THE STOCK IS HIGH. A CONSERVATIVE INVESTOR WOULD LOOK TO SELL IT AT THE EARLIEST OPPORTUNITY.

An ideal example of this is Penn Central (see Figure 27) for which a sell signal was indicated in mid-1968, months before the market itself registered its ultimate bull-market top.

On October 25, 1968, the stock closed at 66¼ and the data on Penn Central was as follows:

Closing price	$66.25
5-week average price	69.82
15-week average price	68.52
40-week average price	69.63

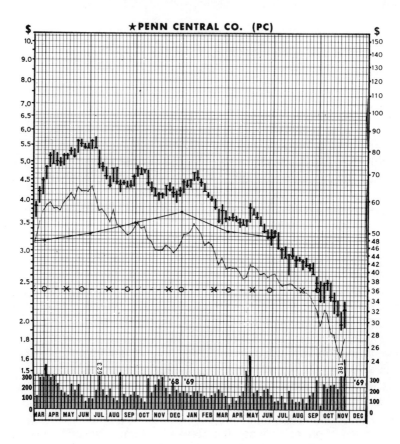

Figure 27 *(Courtesy Securities Research Co.)*

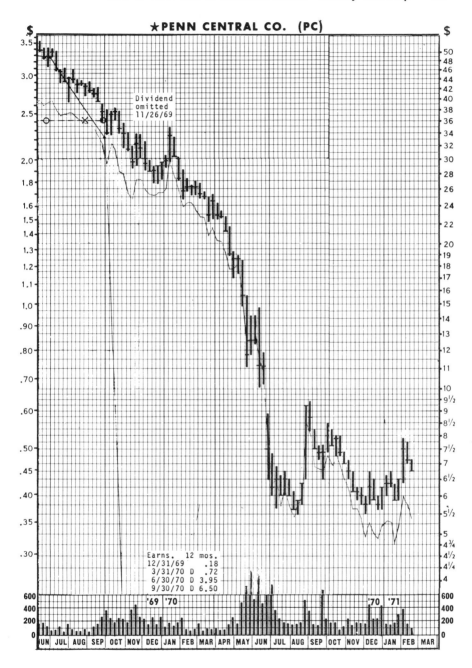

Figure 28 (Courtesy Securities Research Co.)

This was the first week that the 15-week moving average price dropped below the 40-week average price, an action that alerted the investor to prepare to sell the stock. Since the general market was still in an uptrend, the proper procedure in this case was to wait until the stock rallied up into the ideal buying range, this it did three months later, in January, 1969.

Look at Figure 28, to see what subsequently happened to Penn Central stock. The stock subsequently collapsed to a low of about 1 as its monumental problems came to light.

The collapse was based on the huge losses suffered by the company in 1970, which ultimately forced it into receivership in June, 1970. Investigations were undertaken after Penn Central went into bankruptcy. Certain officers and directors of the company were alleged to have benefited by their inside knowledge of the impending bankruptcy while the stock was still up in the $18 range by selling their personal holdings prior to announcement of the bankruptcy.

It is ironic that an investor aware of the importance of timing in regulating his investment decisions and absolutely ignorant of the operations of the company could have sold Penn Central stock over a year and a half earlier at $69.00 or 283 percent higher than the directors, who it is supposed, sold their stock on the basis of inside information.

This is one of the best examples you will ever find of astute timing as the most important single element in the investment selection and decision process.

28. How to Time the Sale of Individual Stocks when the Primary Trend Is Either Down Or Uncertain

When the primary trend is either down or uncertain, the safest course of action to follow in selling a stock differs slightly from that pursued during a bull market. The reason is that stocks often collapse during a bear market without warning. Also, a stock in a downtrend will often fall in price about twice as fast as it rises during a bull market. That is why the rules for selling differ slightly during bear markets.

When the course of the market is uncertain—that is, when the 15-week A-D line is dropping but the intermediate DJI average is still above its 40-week average—a stock should be held as long as its 15-week average remains above the 40-week average. Then he should sell as soon as the stock rallies into the range between the short-term and the long-term average. In other words, the investor sells on the first small rally that comes along. He does not wait for the stock to rally all the way up to the top of the ideal buying range because, if the period of uncertainty turns into a full-scale bear market, the stock may never rally that high.

On the other hand, if the primary trend of the market is definitely down and the intermediate DJI is below the long-term line, one should sell out each position as soon as the 5-week line of each stock falls below the 15-week average. Do not wait for it to drop all the way below the 40-week line or for any rallies to set in. During a bear market, as soon as a stock collapses, sell it, take your cash, and run.

It is possible that the stock might go still higher but the odds are now against it. The averages go down because more stocks are declining than advancing. One's goal, as a conservative investor, is to work in harmony with these declines, not against them. Therefore, instead of holding out to the last possible moment, sell at the first sign of danger, and take a long vacation from the market. Wait until stocks are cheap again and the odds are once more in your favor before you think again of buying.

29. Application of Rules to Buy and Sell

We are now ready to take a stock and show just how the Low-Risk rules are applied in a specific investment situation. We will use Trans World Airlines stock to illustrate precisely how the rules for buying and selling are used in actual practice. Figure 29 shows the price action of TWA that began in October, 1968.

We are assuming that at the point where this chart begins—namely the second week of March, 1968—the 5-, 15-, and 40-week moving averages are all trending up and the stock is being held in an investment portfolio.

The first decision we must make is during the first week of January, 1969, when the 5-week average of $45.02 drops below the 15-week average at $45.75. However, because the direction of the market as measured by the Dow Jones Industrials and the Advance-Decline line is bullish, the correct decision to make is to do nothing at this time. Two weeks later the stock begins to rally, making it appear that the decline was just another one of those pauses that occur periodically during the life of a continuing bull market.

On February 21, 1969, after having rallied to 48¾, the stock closes at 44½ and the 5-week average again turns down. At this time the 5-week average at $46.50 is still above the 15-week average of $46.39, but is so close to dropping below that it will certainly do so at the end of the following week, unless the stock rallies strongly in the meantime.

At the same time, the 15-week DJI average is falling but is still above the 40-week average. Moreover, the A-D line has started to turn down. Because the A-D line is moving down, the possibility exists that a bear market may be about to start. This alerts the investor to review TWA closely preparatory to selling. Nothing was done until April 10, 1969, when the stock closed at 41¼. On this date, the 15-week average at $43.43 for the first time closed below the 40-week moving average, which registered $43.53. At this time the stock was rallying from the high 30's. The investor entered his order to sell the following week when the stock traded between 41¼ and 43¼.

From April 10, 1969, when TWA was at 41¼ until December, 1970, when the stock dropped to less than 10, both the short-term and the 15-week line remained below the 40-week average, indicating that purchase of the stock should have been avoided. In the fall of 1969, both short-term moving averages turned up briefly and it appeared as though a new buy signal might be forthcoming. However, both of them turned down five weeks later without ever rising above the 40-week average.

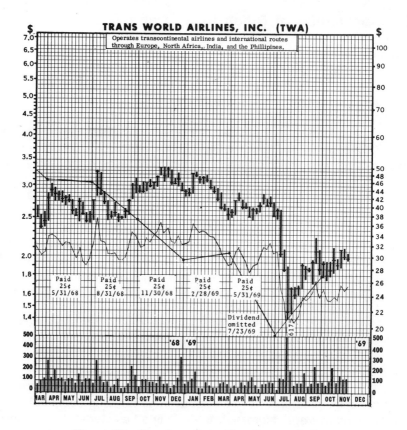

Figure 29 (Courtesy Securities Research Co.)

On January 15, 1971, when TWA closed at 15⅞, its short-term average moved above the 40-week average for the first time in two years. For someone wanting to re-purchase TWA, the Monday following was the day to make that initial purchase. See Figures 30 and 31.

Assuming that TWA was sold according to the sell signal on April 10, 1969, at around 42-43 and then re-purchased two years later at 16, the investor would have been able to buy over 270 shares of TWA for each 100 shares held in 1969. Of course, the actual number of shares re-purchased would have been somewhat less due to the commissions involved first in selling, then re-purchasing the stock, and the capital-gains tax paid on the 1969 profits. Nevertheless, the point is that when

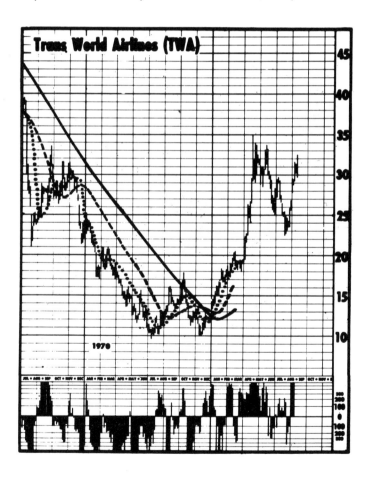

Figure 30   (Courtesy The Worden Tape Reading Studies)

Work Sheet
TRANS WORLD AIRLINES

DATE	PRICE	TAKE AWAY PRICE			5 WEEK		15 WEEK		40 WEEK	
		5 WK	15 WK	40 WK	TOTAL	AVERAGE	TOTAL	AVERAGE	TOTAL	AVERAGE
1970 6-26	11	x	x		63-5/8	$ 12.72	216-1/4	$ 14.42	826-5/8	$ 20.67
7- 2	10-1/2	x	x		61-3/4	12.35	208-7/8	13.92	809-1/8	20.23
10	10-7/8	x	x		58-3/8	11.67	201-7/8	13.46	791-1/8	19.78
17	11-7/8	x	x		57-7/8	11.57	197-1/4	13.15	776	19.40
24	10-7/8	x	x		55-5/8	11.12	191-7/8	12.79	759	18.98
31	12-3/8	x	x		57	11.40	189-1/8	12.61	741-7/8	18.55
8- 7	12-1/2	x	x		59	11.70	187-7/8	12.52	725-3/8	18.13
14	13	x	x		61-1/8	12.12	185-7/8	12.39	708	17.70
21	13-3/4	x	x		63	12.50	185	12.33	691-3/8	17.29
28	15-3/4	x	x		67-7/8	13.47	187-3/8	12.49	677-7/8	16.95
9- 4	14-3/4	x	x		70-1/4	14.05	189-3/8	12.62	663-1/8	16.58
11	13-5/8	x	x		71-3/8	14.27	190-5/8	12.70	649-3/4	16.24
18	14-1/2	x	x		72-3/8	14.57	190-7/8	12.72	640-3/4	16.02
25	14-3/8	x	x		73-1/2	14.70	192-7/8	12.86	631-7/8	15.80
10- 2	16-3/4	x	x		74-1/2	14.90	196-1/2	13.10	624-1/8	15.60
9	15-7/8	x	x		75-5/8	15.02	201-3/8	13.42	616-1/8	15.40
16	13-7/8	x	x		75-7/8	15.17	204-3/4	13.65	607	15.18
23	12-3/8	x	x		74	14.75	206-1/4	13.75	597-5/8	14.94
30	11-3/4	x	x		71-1/8	14.24	206-1/8	13.74	589	14.73
11- 6	12-1/2	x	x		66-7/8	13.37	207-3/4	13.85	584-1/8	14.60
13	12-1/4	x	x		63-1/4	12.65	207-5/8	13.84	578-1/4	14.46
20	10-7/8	x	x		60-1/4	11.95	206	13.73	568-3/8	14.21
27	10-3/8	x			58-1/4	11.65	203-3/8	13.56	559-7/8	14.00
12- 4	12-3/8	x			58-7/8	11.77	202	13.47	551-3/4	13.79
11	12-1/8	x			58-1/2	11.70	198-3/8	13.22	544-3/8	13.61
18	12-1/8	x			58-3/8	11.67	195-3/4	13.05	538-1/4	13.45
24	12-1/2	x			59-1/2	11.90	194-5/8	12.97	532-7/8	13.32
31	13-3/4	x			62-7/8	12.52	193-7/8	12.91	528-3/4	13.21
1971 1- 8	14-3/8	x			64-7/8	12.97	193-7/8	12.91	526-5/8	13.16
15	15-7/8	x			68-5/8	13.72	193	12.87	526-1/4	13.15
22	16-1/2	x			73	14.60	193-5/8	12.91	527-5/8	13.19
29	18	x			78-1/2	15.70	197-3/4	13.19	531-7/8	13.29
2- 5	16-7/8				81-5/8	16.32	202-1/4	13.49	533-3/4	13.34
11	18				85-1/4	17.05	208-1/2	13.90	532-1/8	13.43
19	17-3/4				87-1/8	17.42	213-3/4	14.25	541-1/2	13.54
26	18-7/8				89-1/2	17.90	220-3/8	14.69	547-5/8	13.69
3 - 5	20-3/8				91-7/8	18.37	229-7/8	15.32	555-5/8	13.89

Figure 31

an investor follows a procedure such as this, which is designed for both buying and selling according to predetermined guidelines, he will end up holding enough additional shares of stock to more than make up for the effect of taxes and the erosive action of inflation.

On the other hand, an investor who did not sell but merely held on to his TWA stock throughout the 1969-70 bear market had to wait until 1972 to see the stock at the $50 level again. But the investor who re-bought TWA in 1971 at $16 a share was able to show another good profit.

Timing then is one key to consistent Low-Risk stock-market profits. And a dependable cyclical stock that moves between $15 and $40 every three or four years will often serve the investor better than the one growth stock in a thousand that is worth buying and holding through a lifetime.

PART VI

How Well Does It Work?

30. Illustrations Using the Low Risk Method over Extended Time Periods

We have now progressed to the point where—by using the rules that have been developed up to this point—it is possible to show how the Low-Risk Method performs over an extended period of time. We will illustrate these procedures in two different ways. First we will work with three stocks each possessing radically different trading characteristics. Then we will apply the Low Risk Method to illustrate how to manage an investment portfolio working from a Master Investment List.

The stocks are Boeing Co., Brunswick Corp., and U.S. Steel Corp. Our illustrations of Boeing and U.S. Steel begin in January, 1962 and cover fourteen years. The Brunswick stock spans a 23-year period that commences in 1953.

In January, 1962, the bear market that ended in June of that year was just becoming visible to the majority of investors. Both Boeing and U.S. Steel had already been sold. Our tracking period begins, therefore, with these two stocks, and most others, in a bear market, and with investors seeking to make purchases as they are signaled by the Low-Risk investing method. From the initial point of purchase, we will continue to track these stocks through 1976, buying them each time we get a Low-Risk purchase signal and selling when the indications we receive dictate such action.

The Brunswick example takes in a more extensive period. It illustrates several different activity characteristics during the 23-year span that we would otherwise have had to use at least one or two more examples to examine. Brunswick offers valuable insight into the effect of the changing evaluation of both fundamentals and expectations under changing market conditions on both the market price and the results of this method.

The results achieved in these three long-range examples are indeed startling. They speak loudly and eloquently for the Low-Risk Method, and prove that often it is not what you buy but when you buy that can make all the difference.

For example, in November, 1963, at the time of the first purchase signal in Boeing, the stock was trading at 19⅛. At the time of the last buy signal in March, 1975, it traded at 18½. In other words, during these twelve years and despite some extremely big price swings the price of Boeing was virtually unchanged. But an investor following the Low-Risk Method of investing would have netted a $13,995 return on an original investment of only $1,912.50! He could do this because he was able to capture big portions of each of Boeing's price swings when there were such swings.

Then, by re-investing these profits in combination with the emphasis placed on proper timing, the investor's original investment would pyramid sufficiently by March, 1975, to enable him to purchase 350 shares for each 100 shares he originally held.

The average annual profit realized on this investment would be 56 percent. To achieve these extraordinary results, the investor would not have to spend an inordinate amount of time following Boeing, studying its operations, etc. On the contrary, he had only to devote one minute per week to keeping his three Low-Risk moving averages on Boeing current.

Furthermore, he would not have to trade furiously to achieve these results. In fact, he'd hardly have to trade at all. It was only necessary to make seven purchases in the 12-year period.

Similar excellent results were noted with Brunswick. In this case the stock itself showed an excellent rate of appreciation between the first and last buy signals. At the time of the first buy signal in January, 1956, Brunswick was trading at 1½; at the time of the last buy signal in February, 1976, the stock was 13⅞.

The appreciation was a handsome 900 percent but it was as nothing compared to the $21,059 captured using the Low-Risk Method— despite the fact that three of the seven purchases made and completed during this 23-year period were subsequently sold at losses!

Again, with re-investment of these profits in combination with capitalization of the price swings, the original $150 had grown sufficiently to purchase 1365 shares on the most recent signal date.

Our third example illustrates the value of Low-Risk investment methods during even the most adverse market conditions. U.S. Steel had been in a long-term uninterrupted downtrend throughout the entire decade of the sixties. To make matters more difficult, the stock did not have even one swing during this entire period that was really worth capturing.

From a high of almost 110 in 1959, the stock dropped to about 25 in 1971. Despite this abysmal performance, the stock finally did turn the bend in 1973. Those investors who purchased U.S. Steel on its most recent buy signals in October, 1973 and again in January, 1975 were rewarded with profits of over $4,000.

31. Boeing Corp.

Historically Boeing has been ideally suited to the Low-Risk concept of investing, and continues to give evidence of remaining so in the future.

The company is big. It is one of the giants of American industry. There are well over 21 million shares outstanding and the stock is always active. This means it is almost always possible to buy or sell a fair quantity of stock quickly and without disrupting the market.

Until recently, the company produced a limited product line that it sold to two large categories of customers, the Government and the airlines industry. Boeing is a world leader in the manufacture of commercial aircraft with its 707's, 727's and 747's, and their customers tend to buy its products in spurts. Because of the high unit cost of each sale, these buying spurts build Boeing's sales up by many millions of dollars. On the other hand, the company has always been vulnerable to abrupt cancellations, stretchings out of deliveries, or the preemption of its product leadership by the competition.

This, of course, creates difficulty for Boeing's management because it puts tremendous pressures on it to manage well during peak business periods and then to survive during the company's periodic famines. It is a tribute to the management that it has proved competent to do both. While the nature of Boeing's business makes the company difficult to manage, the stock is an ideal choice for an investor seeking dependable cyclical stocks for, with its feast-or-famine nature, the stock is susceptible to overdiscounting during both bull and bear markets.

When the company announces a new product such as the 747, the stock generally becomes overvalued, especially during bull markets. Then, when the product runs into unforeseen difficulties or if major projects are cancelled, the stock collapses in price to a level far below its worth.

A look at Boeing's chart in Figure 32 shows how well its price follows the company's operating results. During the early years shown on the chart, the correlationship was fairly precise as each new generation of commercial aircraft brought higher levels of profits. The spurt of 707 sales in the early 1960's saw profits rise from 70 cents to $2.40 a share. The advent of the 727's generated a profit rise from $1.25 to $5.75. With each successive upthrust in profits, the price of Boeing stock also rose in reflection of its corporate success. The stock went from 12 to 28 in the 1960-62 period and from 16 to 90 between 1962 and 1966.

It was understandable, therefore, that some investors would attempt

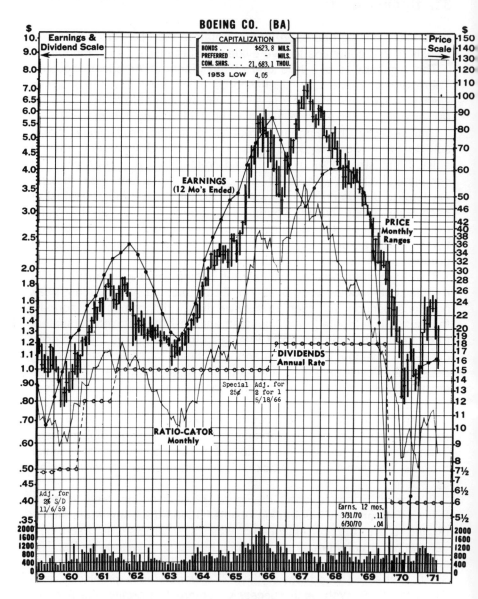

Figure 32 (Courtesy Securities Research Co.)

to discount the success they foresaw for the 747 and the SST programs by bidding Boeing up to 110 in 1967. However, the SST program was scrapped in 1971 and the 747 program became a fiasco and almost a disaster. There were delays in delivery because the supplier of the engines had trouble meeting specifications, and there were operational delays upon delivery while the inevitable bugs were worked out. Some passengers were apprehensive about riding the plane because of its huge size. Then, along came tight money, layoffs, and a recession—people in droves stopped traveling. Consequently, airlines postponed deliveries of aircraft into the future in order to conserve cash.

The realities of Boeing's operations and investor anticipations of

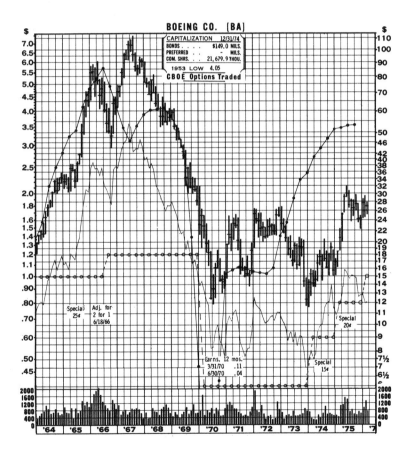

Figure 32a

them are both reflected in the price of the stock. Prices in turn traced a pattern that could easily have been harnessed by a Low-Risk investor for his benefit. From 1960 through 1965, Boeing's price closely followed the company's operating results. When earnings rose, the price of the stock rose. When earnings fell, the stock fell. Then from 1966 through 1968, the anticipation of what was expected to happen carried more weight than current results and the price of the stock outdistanced earnings both up and down.

Along with the decline in 1966 of the general market, Boeing fell from 90 to 44 in anticipation of the slack period between the phasing out of the 727 program and the start of the 747 program. The stock fell over 50 percent even though reported earnings were rising.

Late in 1966, coupled with the end of the market decline, Boeing began to rise dramatically from 44 to 110 in anticipation of the 747 program despite a rapid fall in earnings during this period. When earnings again turned up in the third quarter of 1967, enough investors had already foreseen problems with the 747 to precipitate the decline in Boeing stock, which did not end until the third quarter of 1970.

Here is a summary of how an investor who had the assistance of the signals generated by the Low-Risk Method of Successful Investing would have fared during this thirteen-year period.

In December, 1961, just before our study begins, the 15-week average price of Boeing dropped below the 40-week price, alerting the investor of an impending change of trend. The investor, anticipating this change in trend, sold his Boeing stock in January, 1962, at 26 on a rally that subsequently carried the stock above 28.

When the bear market of 1962 came to an end in June, 1962, Boeing did not rally along with most other stocks, but instead continued in a private bear market of its own for another year. It subsequently made its bear-market bottom in July, 1963, at 15½. From here, it recovered slowly and did not register a buy signal until November, 1963, at 19⅛. This signal occurred when the five-week moving average of Boeing rose above the 40-week average price at a time when both the 15-week Advance-Decline line and the Dow Jones industrial average were moving up.

After its buy signal in 1963, the stock gave no further action signals until 1966. A period of hesitation in the 30-36 range began in September, 1964, and continued through 1965. During this "congestion" period, in July, 1965, the 5-week M/A dropped below the 40-week line temporarily. However, no selling was called for since both market wide indexes were moving up at the time. Instead this was an appropriate point at which an investor with money to spare might have considered making additional purchases. The stock was at 35½.

In retrospect, it is clear that the fall of the five-week average below the 40-week line during a bull market often signals the end of a period of congestion. At the time of its occurrence, however, an investor is rarely so confident, because events surrounding such periods of congestion give him ample reason to suspect the stock will turn down rather than continue in its bull market. For this reason, an investor needs something like the Low-Risk Method to remind him forcefully that the probabilities continue to favor higher prices.

A few days later, Boeing resumed its advance and didn't stop until the stock was at 90. Then in June, 1966, the five-week average again fell below the 40-week line. This time, however, the general market lines were also trending down. Boeing was therefore sold at 73¾ on a rally that subsequently carried to 78.

In October, 1966, Boeing sold down to 42. It made a "V" type recovery that moved so swiftly that a buy was not signaled until January, 1967, at 66. This recovery continued, uninterrupted, to 110 before reacting. The reaction caused the 5-week line to pass through the 40-week average on October, 1967. Since the market wide indexes were still favorable, this penetration required no action unless the investor wanted to buy additional stock at 81.

In November, the 15-week average penetrated the 40-week average. Although at this point the overall market still seemed healthy, the fact that Boeing was acting so poorly was an ominous sign and, according to our rules, preparations were begun to sell the stock at 92. This sale was consummated in December, 1967, as the stock rallied to 94 just before beginning a bear-market decline that was to last three full years.

The market decline begun in November, 1967, did not end until July, 1970, when Boeing traded briefly at 11⅞. It thereupon began a recovery that culminated in a buy signal on January, 1971. From here the stock swiftly moved to $24 where it stalled for several months. Then, with equal rapidity, it dropped back to $14. On the decline a signal to sell was given in August, 1971 at $16¼ causing a loss of $1,179.38.

During the next two years three more buy signals were recorded. In January, 1972 at $21⅜; November, 1972 at 23⅜; and October, 1973 at $19¾. The January, 1972 purchase was closed out at a nominal $315 profit while the other two resulted in losses of about $1,300 each. The final purchase, made in March, 1975 at $18½ was closed out on December 31, 1976 at $44¾.

The signals we have discussed would have guided a Low Risk Investor following Boeing to enter the orders shown below with the following results.

STATEMENT OF ACTIVITY
(Boeing Corp.)

Date	Order	Quantity	Price	Debit	Credit	Realized Profit
Nov., 1963	Buy	100	19⅛	$ 1,912.50		
June, 1966	Sell	100	73¾		$ 7,375.00	$ 5,462.50
Jan., 1967	Buy	110	66	7,260.00		
Dec., 1967	Sell	110	92		10,120.00	2,860.00
Jan., 1971	Buy	555	18⅜	10,198.12		
Aug., 1971	Sell	555	16¼		9,018.75	(1,179.38)
Jan., 1972	Buy	420	21⅜	8,977.50		
Sept., 1972	Sell	420	22⅛		9,292.50	315.00
Nov., 1972	Buy	400	23⅜	9,350.00		
Apr., 1973	Sell	400	20⅛		8,050.00	(1,300.00)
Oct., 1973	Buy	400	19¾	7,900.00		
Nov., 1973	Sell	400	16⅜		6,550.00	(1,350.00)
Mar., 1975	Buy	350	18½	6,475.00		
Dec., 1976	Sell	350	44¾		15,662.50	9,187.50

Net profits realized on 7 completed transaction $13,995.62

Average annual return Nov., 1963 - Dec., 1976 (13 years 2 months) $1,062.96

Percent average annual return on original investment...56%

Note how the amount of stock an investor can buy often grows with each successive purchase. The reason for this is due to the pyramiding effects of the Low-Risk Method and the way it capitalizes on making purchases near market bottoms.

The $7,375 realized from the sale of 100 Boeing shares in June, 1966, when the stock was 73¾ was sufficient to purchase almost 112 shares when the price dropped to 66. For illustrative purposes, however, and to simplify the examples, all purchases have been rounded off to the nearest lower unit of five shares.

The second Boeing investment realized a smaller monetary profit ($2,860) than the first, but the bear market that followed was much more severe, thereby permitting the purchase of over 5 shares for each share sold in 1967.

This proves as well as anything can that properly harnessed bear markets are just as vital an element in building capital as bull markets. Bear markets get the price of stocks down to such bargain levels that your bull-market profits can often buy at least twice the stock for the same amount of money.

It should also be pointed out here that the investor's return on his original $1,912.50 investment could in actual practice have been much more than the amount shown above. The preceding illustration assumes the investor's capital was employed only to buy Boeing stock but, as you can see, the investor's money was out of the market for 23 months between January, 1962, and November, 1963; for six months between June, 1966, and January, 1967; for three years between December, 1967, and January, 1971 as well as similar interludes from 1972 through 1975.

In other words, the capital so employed was lying dormant for over half the review period. *All the capital growth came not in a thirteen year span but in just seven years and two months!* Therefore, the annual percentage return shown above was not 56 percent but almost twice that amount, adjusting for the amount of time the money was actually invested.

There is an excellent possibility as we will soon see that a Low-Risk investor with a sufficiently diversified master selection list could have found another stock in which to invest, while waiting for the next buying opportunity in Boeing to present itself.

32. Brunswick Corp.

Our second example, Brunswick Corp., exemplifies a number of different characteristics, as shown in Figure 33.

First, during much of the 1950's Brunswick was the kind of super-growth stock that every investor dreams of buying right at the bottom and holding all the way to the top. The stock went from 68 cents in 1953 to $75 in just a little over seven years.

The motivating force propelling this move was the development of an automatic pinsetting machine for bowling alleys together with a phenomenal growth of bowling alleys between 1955 and 1960. Regardless of how fast the stock advanced, Brunswick's ability to install its pinsetters permitted earnings to advance even faster. In 1960 the momentum of the price advance in Brunswick's stock finally began to outpace the momentum of the advance in Brunswick's earnings.

This first Brunswick chart highlights several things, the most important of which is that if you are so fortunate as to find yourself owning a dynamic stock such as Brunswick during this period in its history, the Low-Risk Method will keep you invested in the stock for the entire duration of its bull market and will get you out very near the top.

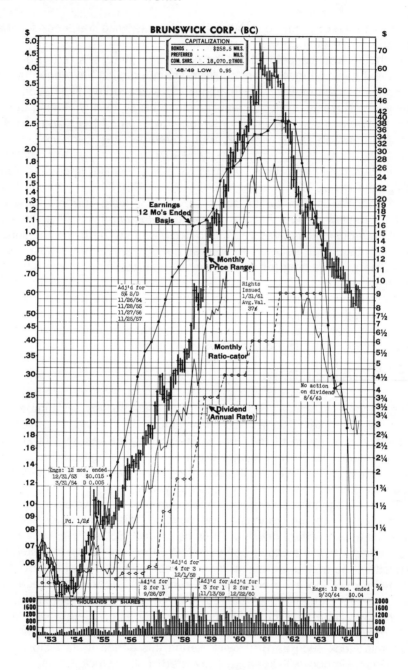

BRUNSWICK CORP. (BC)

Figure 33   *(Courtesy Securities Research Co.)*

The only hesitation in Brunswick's advance came in 1955. Assuming a purchase was made at the end of 1955 at 1½, the Low-Risk Method kept the investor in Brunswick until July, 1961, when it signaled a sale at 56 after the stock had sold as high as 75.

This period in Brunswick's history illustrates another point: When a strong, fundamentally grounded move takes place within a stock or an industry, the move that such a development generates lasts longer and causes a stock to go further than anyone dares to estimate in the beginning. Furthermore, the moves are likely to be so strong that they will negate temporarily the tendency of the stock to act in harmony with general market conditions.

Finally, Brunswick illustrates that just as a stock sometimes has a tendency toward undervaluation, it can often turn around to become equally overvalued when its value becomes recognized by the mass body of investors.

After the phenomenal rise, Brunswick proved itself unequal to its task. Eager to expand before competitors caught up, the company over-expanded and thoroughly oversaturated the market. Many installations were made at locations uneconomic to the high-priced automatic pinsetters and in otherwise good areas that had been inundated with too many bowling alleys. As a result, many alleys soon found themselves in receivership, and Brunswick itself took over the operation of more and more alleys.

With this, earnings plummeted (see Figure 34) and, in place of a $2.50 level of earnings in 1961, Brunswick reported a $4.21 per share deficit in 1965.

While the company struggled to regain its balance in 1967, the stock plunged from its all-time high of 75 in 1961 to 6½. It is again significant that the Low-Risk Method kept an investor out of Brunswick from the time it flashed its signal to sell at 56 in 1961 down to 9¾ in 1965, thus protecting the investor from most of the decline.

During the two-year period from late 1964 through 1966, Brunswick traded in a very narrow price range most of the time. It seldom traded below 8 or above 11. This was a period of low-amplitude movement in the price pattern similar to that which the investor was cautioned to avoid with many utilities. Occasionally the stock traded above 11 and, as noted, it sold as low as 6½ in 1967. For the most part, however, it was in the narrow trading range that reflected indecision and a hands-off attitude on the part of investors. They were waiting to see whether Brunswick's management would successfully overcome its difficulties.

This narrow amplitude of the trading range made it difficult for the Low-Risk investor to catch the swings correctly. Consequently, he found himself caught with two consecutive losses as the stock whip-sawed back and forth indecisively. Both losses were limited, as losses with the Low-Risk Method are designed to be. The first loss was ⅝ point; the second, exactly one point. Nevertheless, with two consecutive losses out of the first four completed transactions, the stock still returned an average profit of over 418 percent per year.

By 1967, management was demonstrating that it could once more

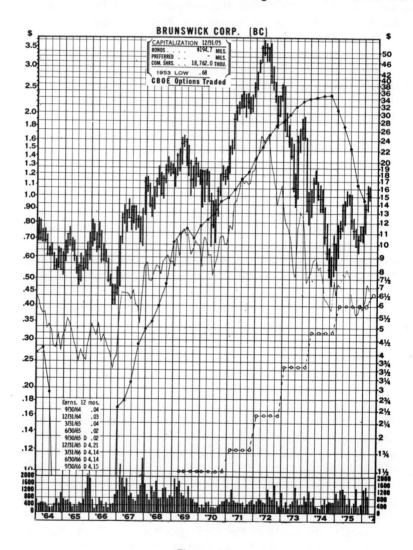

Figure 34

make Brunswick a strong, viable, profitable operation and, in line with this, the stock's Low-Risk signals again became consistently reliable. The buy signal that flashed in January, 1967, at 9¼ carried a Brunswick investment through September, 1969, at which point the stock was sold at 19½.

Brunswick then performed very favorably during the 1969-70 bear market, declining much less than the average stock. It flashed a buy signal in August, 1970, at 16⅞ which was closed out at 37⅝. Then came two more purchase signals, one of which was closed out at a small loss, the second at a small profit.

It is not necessary to follow this stock through each potential action signal. The reader by now undoubtedly has a good idea from reading our previous illustrations what factors are considered at each decision point and how they are evaluated. It is sufficient merely to show a statement of results arising from the actions taken.

STATEMENT OF ACTIVITY
(Brunswick Corp.)

Date	Order	Quantity	Price	Debit	Credit	Realized Profit
Jan., 1956	Buy	100	1½	$ 150.00		
July., 1961	Sell	100	56		$ 5,600.00	$ 5,450.00
Jan., 1965	Buy	570	9¾	5,557.00		
Aug., 1965	Sell	570	9⅛		5,201.25	(355.75)
Dec., 1965	Buy	485	10⅛	5,153.25		
June., 1966	Sell	485	9⅝		4,668.25	(485.00)
June., 1967	Buy	510	9¼	4,717.50		
Sept., 1969	Sell	510	19½		9,945.00	5,227.50
Aug., 1970	Buy	590	16⅞	9,956.25		
Sept., 1970	Sell	590	37⅝		22,198.75	12,242.50
Feb., 1975	Buy	1850	12	22,200.00		
Sept., 1975	Sell	1850	10¼		18,962.50	(3,237.50)
Feb., 1976	Buy	1365	13⅞	18,939.37		
Oct., 1976	Sell	1365	15½		21,157.50	2,218.12

Net realized profits on the seven completed transactions $21,059.87

Average annual return Jan., 1956 - Oct., 1976 (21 years 10 months)..........$964.57

Average percentage return on original investment 643.0%

In this case, note several things. Observe first how the quantity of stock you can buy pyramids when you sell out at a big profit and then buy back at a lower price later. Then notice how, even though this is true, a severe bear market is more useful to the technique than just a mild one. In 1965, after a decline from 56 to 9¾, a Low-Risk investor could purchase 5.7 shares of Brunswick for each share he previously owned. In August, 1970, however, following the much milder bear market for Brunswick, the stock dropped from 19½ to 16⅞ and a Low-Risk buyer could purchase only 1.15 shares for each share previously held. Again, this points out that the results you are liable to get from the Low-Risk Method is a function of the volatility of the stock. The more widely it moves, the better your investment results are likely to be.

This example points out also the corrosive effects of even small losses in preventing the total share holdings from building up. It shows also that even if an investor is right just 50 percent of the time, he can still turn in a fantastic performance record—provided that his profits are big when he is right and he can find a way to limit his losses when he is wrong. The profits shown here were as high as 3,633 percent, while the losses were limited to less than 15 percent.

As with Boeing, here, too, the investor was out of Brunswick for significant periods of time, especially in the interval between July, 1961, and January, 1965. Thus, rather than remaining dormant, the profits generated by the first Brunswick sale could productively have been utilized in the bull market that began in mid-1962 to generate additional profits.

33. U.S. Steel Corp.

The final stock we have selected for illustrative purposes is U.S. Steel Corp. This stock was chosen because it appeared to be one of the most difficult examples with which to test the reliability of the Low-Risk Method. As we shall see with the help of Figures 35 and 36, the method performed admirably.

U.S. Steel was one of the most difficult stocks with which to make money during the decade of the sixties. While the Dow Jones Industrials were speeding toward 1,000 and thousands of stocks were doubling, tripling and quadrupling in value, the eminent blue chip, U.S. Steel, was in a long-term bear market of its own that took it from an all-time high of 100 in 1959 down to 25 in 1971.

The reasons for this were not to be found solely in earnings. In 1973, when U.S. Steel was selling at 28, its reported earnings were higher than in 1960 when the stock was trading in the eighties. Nor were the answers to be found in deterioration of plant and equipment, for during the past fifteen years U.S. Steel had spent more money on new plant and equipment per share than the stock was selling for late in 1971.

Instead the stock appears to have been in a bear market because a rapid rise in its labor costs and the high costs of its plant modernization have combined to limit the company's ability to increase its earnings. It has also placed it at a competitive disadvantage internationally, so much so that a Japanese steel company replaced U.S. Steel as the largest steel company in the world. To add insult to injury, purchasing-agent friends in the steel industry report that the Japanese are willing to sell them steel products at less than their own company's cost of manufacturing.

The implications of these and other potentially unfavorable developments caused investors to value U.S. Steel at a lower price than fundamentals would otherwise dictate.

This was a real challenge to the Low-Risk Method. What would happen with a stock such as U.S. Steel, which had rewarded its faithful

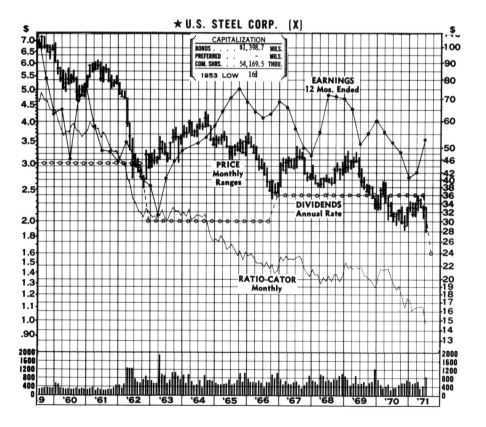

Figure 35 *(Courtesy Securities Research Co.)*

long-term holders with a 75 percent shrinkage in value in return for twelve years of patience? Would the Low-Risk Method also show a loss or would it show a profit? If the stock did show a profit, would it be sufficiently large or merely a token profit?

After completing and reviewing the statistics, we can conclude that the Low-Risk Method performed admirably well, all things considered, although not nearly as well as it did with the other two stocks.

The Low-Risk Method gave nine buy signals in U.S. Steel. The first occurred in October, 1962, at $47; and the last, in January, 1975, at 47¼. Of these signals, four were closed out at a profit.

Finally, after struggling to achieve a higher rate of earnings for years everything seemed to come together in 1972. From that point, in just three years, the level of U.S. Steel earnings skyrocketed almost sevenfold from $2.00 per share in 1972 to $13.43 in 1975. And to the stockholders' delight, the price of the stock followed earnings, going from $27 to $90. As a result, the last two Low-Risk investments in U.S. Steel have resulted in profits of $4,035.25 suggesting that perhaps

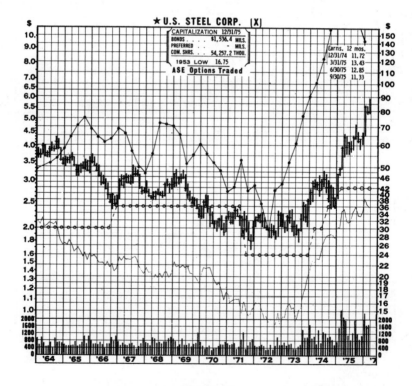

Figure 36

after a drought of more than a decade, the stock will once more profitably react to our Low-Risk Method signals.

The following table summarizes the results:

STATEMENT OF ACTIVITY
(U.S. Steel Corp.)

Date	Order	Quantity	Price	Debit	Credit	Realized Profit
Oct., 1962	Buy	100	47	$4,700.00		
Jan., 1965	Sell	100	54		$5,400.00	$ 700.00
Dec., 1965	Buy	100	53½	5,350.00		
Mar., 1966	Sell	100	49		4,900.00	(450.00)
Jan., 1967	Buy	110	44	4,840.00		
June, 1968	Sell	110	44		4,840.00	—
Sept., 1968	Buy	115	41½	4,772.50		
June, 1969	Sell	115	45		5,175.00	402.50
Jan., 1971	Buy	160	33¼	5,320.00		
Aug., 1971	Sell	160	28¼		4,520.00	(800.00)
Jan., 1972	Buy	140	31⅜	4,392.50		
July, 1972	Sell	140	29⅛		4,077.50	(315.00)
Nov., 1972	Buy	120	33¼	3,990.00		
Jan., 1973	Sell	120	31¾		3,810.00	(180.00)
Oct., 1973	Buy	105	35¼	3,701.00		
June, 1974	Sell	105	44¾		4,698.75	997.75
Jan., 1975	Buy	100	47¼	4,725.00		
Sept, 1976	Sell	150*	51¾		7,762.50	3,037.50

Net realized profits on the nine completed transactions $3,392.75

Average annual return October 1962 - June 1976 (14 years 9 months)... $ 242.34

Percent average annual return on original investment 5.2%

*Due to 3 for 2 stock split.

34. USING THE LOW RISK METHOD WITH A MASTER INVESTMENT LIST OVER AN EXTENDED PERIOD OF TIME

We have seen how the Low Risk Method performs over an extended period of time when an investor determines in advance to buy and sell a particular stock each time a Low Risk signal is given. If, the investor had chosen a stock such as Brunswick or Boeing, the method would have performed superbly. If, on the other hand, a typical utility stock or a stock like U.S. Steel had been chosen the results were likely to be disappointing.

In real life most investors do not pick a stock in advance and say they will buy it when they get a Low Risk signal. Instead they buy a stock that looks like it is "about to move" when they are ready to buy. That is the function of a Master Investment List as discussed on page 57. With such a list, purchases can be made from among the strongest stocks according to the rules explained in the book. Here is a sample of the success possible by working with such a list.

For our Master Investment List we have chosen a group of 20 stocks that in 1973 were said to be among the stocks most favored by large institutional investors. It is not quite certain just what criteria were used to determine that these were the institutional favorites since there were many other stocks more widely held by institutions than some on this list. Nevertheless the list was independently prepared by Weiseneberger Investors Services and so I can't be criticized for picking stocks that would "look good" using the Low Risk Method. It is sufficiently diversified to serve as a Master Investment List. And, while it is large enough to test the ideas in this book, it is small enough that we could do all the necessary computations within a reasonable period of time.

The first thing we did was to see what might have happened if someone had merely bought each stock on this list on January 1, 1970; then held on until December 31, 1976 at which point all the stocks were sold. the results are shown below. Anyone who held on for the full period would have just barely broken even. If they had originally bought 100 shares of each of the 20 stocks they would have paid $119,450. After seven years, these same stocks were worth just $120,125, a profit of only $675.

Twenty Institutional Favorite Stocks
Aggregate Performance if Bought on 1/1/70 and Held Until 12/31/76

	Price 1/1/70	Price 12/31/76	$ Gain or Loss	% Gain or Loss
American Home Products (3/1)	$24.00	$ 32.00	$ 8.00	33.3 %
AMP Inc. (3/1)	18.62	28.25	9.63	51.7
Avon Products (2/1)	86.50	49.50	(37.00)	(42.8)
Coca Cola	82.50	79.00	(3.50)	(4.2)
Dr. Pepper (3/1)(2/1)	7.75	14.25	6.50	83.9
Dun & Bradstreet (2/1)	29.25	30.50	1.25	4.3
Eastman Kodak	82.00	86.00	4.00	4.9
IBM Corp.	286.63	279.13	(7.50)	(2.6)
Int'l Flavors (3/2)(2/1)	20.75	22.12	1.37	6.6
Johnson & Johnson (3/1)	60.00	78.00	18.00	30.0
Lubrizol Corp. (2/1)	31.00	36.00	5.00	16.1
Merck & Co. (2/1)	57.00	68.12	11.12	19.5
Minn. Mining & Mfg. (2/1)	54.88	56.63	1.75	3.2
Pfizer, Inc. (3/1)	34.37	29.37	(5.00)	(14.5)
Proctor & Gamble (2/1)	54.50	93.63	39.13	71.8

	Price 1/1/70	Price 12/31/76	$ Gain or Loss	% Gain or Loss
Schering - Plough (2/1)	29.00	44.75	15.75	54.3
Sears Roebuck	68.00	69.00	1.00	1.5
Simplicity Pattern (3/1)	27.75	15.62	(12.13)	(43.7)
Warner Lambert Co. (2/1)	35.00	30.88	(4.12)	(11.8)
Xerox Corp.	105.00	58.50	(46.50)	(44.3)
	$1,194.50	$1,201.25	$ 6.75	0.6 %

NOTE: All the prices shown above are adjusted for any stock splits that may have occurred during the period of the test. If there were any, the size of the stock split is shown in the parenthesis. Thus (2/1) means that there was a two for one stock split in the stock some time during the period of the test.

That wasn't so good. So next we looked at how the institutions who owned the stocks fared. With their professional management, their access to high priced research reports and possibly even inside information, they should have done much better.

To do this we had to refer to a publication known as the *Stock Guide* published each month by Standard & Poors' Corporation. One of the things the *Stock Guide* lists is the number of financial institutions that own every stock as well as the total number of shares they owned in the previous month. The number of institutions surveyed is 2,000 including investment companies and insurance companies. In other words, what the *Stock Guide* shows is the total investment activity of all the people who get paid for managing other people's money. These are the people who are supposed to be the smartest investors in the world.

One of the stocks they favored was American Home Products Corp. To show how we went about determining what the institutions did. Here in the first three columns is what we found in the *Stock Guide* for American Home Products in 1970.

EOM Price is the price of American Home Products stock at the End Of each Month.

The third column shows the institutional holdings reported by the *Stock Guide*. These are the holdings for each stock with the final three zeros omitted. Therefore the January figure of 3,878 actually means that institutions held 3,878,000 shares of the stock at the end of the month rounded off to the nearest thousand. Also all these figures shown are lagged one month. That is, the number shown for January was actually reported in the *Stock Guide* in February to conform with when the trades actually took place.

Then in column 4 we computed how the institutional holdings changed each month from the month before. In February, for example, they owned 19,000 less shares of American Home Products than in January. This means that although some institutions might have bought the stock during January, others sold enough so that when all the buys and sells were added together the group sold 19,000 shares more than it bought. Since we didn't know how much they received for the stock we made a guess by estimating that on balance the price they got was probably somewhere in between the price of the stock at the end of January (64⅝) and the price at the end of February (67). These two prices were first averaged together, then divided by 2, to get an average price of $65.8125 which was then multiplied by the number of shares sold, (19). This gives a rough estimate of how much the institutions probably received for the stock they sold during the month.

Month	EOM Price	Institu- tional Holdings	Net Change for Month	Value of Institutional	
				Purchases	Sales
Dec., 1969	72				
Jan., 1970	64⅝	3,878			
Feb.	67	3,859	(19)		$ 1,250.44
Mar.	63½	3,976	117	$ 7,634.25	
Apr.	59	3,872	(104)		6,370.00
May	57⅞	3,813	(59)		3,447.81
June	57	3,815	2	114.87	
July	55⅞	3,867	52	2,934.75	
Aug.	56	4,109	242	13,536.88	
Sept.	62⅝	4,107	(2)		118.63
Oct.	63⅞	4,097	(10)		632.50
Nov.	67¼	3,736	(361)		23,668.06
Dec.	70¾	3,665	(71)		4,899.00
			(213)		

The cost of buying back these 213 shares on 12/31/70 at 70¾ was $15,069.75

The Total Value of Institutional Purchases and Sales was $39,290.50 $40,386.44

On these purchases and sales they made a profit of $ 1,095.94

Which on a percentage basis came to   2.8%

In contrast the price of the stock dropped from 72 to 70¾ during the year resulting in a loss of   (1.7%)

Then at the end of December 1976 all these monthly net changes for the previous six years were added together. If during the seven years institutions bought more stock then they sold this figure would be a plus. If they sold more it would be a minus.

In the illustration above for 1970, institutions sold 213,000 shares more than they bought. If our experiment had lasted just one year instead of seven we would have closed out the position by buying back the stock at the end of December at 70¾.

Having done this for each of the 20 stocks showed us how well the institutions fared during this 7-year period.

Twenty Institutional Favorite Stocks
Aggregate Performance Record of Approximately 2,000 Institutions
January 1, 1970 - December 31, 1976

	Net Change in Holdings	Sum of Purchases	Sum of Sales	Aggregate Profit (loss)	%
American Home Products	(2,196)	$275,184.06	$268,636.81	$(6,547.25)	(2.4)%
AMP Inc.	(2,665)	149,696.81	181,494.50	31,797.69	21.2
Avon Products	387	530,367.56	460,864.50	(69,503.06)	(13.1)
Coca Cola	61	208,139.75	197,939.19	(10,200.56)	(4.9)
Dr. Pepper	(658)	73,549.43	43,254.30	(30,295.13)	(41.2)
Dun & Bradstreet	252	98,599.50	79,330.81	(19,268.69)	(19.5)
Eastman Kodak	1,210	478,658.62	461,809.25	(16,849.37)	(3.5)
IBM	l,996	2,045,277.44	1,973,877.31	(71,400.13)	(3.5)
Int'l Flav & Fragrances	70	83,614.93	74,439.68	(9,175.25)	(11.0)
Johnson & Johnson	2,737	446,195.50	346,659.25	(99,536.25)	(22.3)
Lubrizol Corp.	2,074	161,006.25	154,209.43	(6,796.82)	(4.2)
Merck & Co.	(668)	423,761.92	378,730.31	(45,031.61)	(10.6)
Minnesota Mining & Mfg.	(433)	372,025.50	342,065.75	(29,959.75)	(8.1)
Pfizer, Inc.	1,121	244,865.87	218,965.12	(25,900.75)	(10.6)
Proctor & Gamble	(2,541)	311,598.37	382,137.62	70,539.25	22.6
Schering-Plough, Inc.	(1,604)	272,724.37	275,844.75	3,120.38	1.1
Sears Roebuck	333	332,593.44	373,550.62	40,957.18	12.3
Simplicity Pattern	168	69,317.12	69,716.62	399.50	0.6
Warner Lambert Co.	2,387	287,902.87	260,632.43	(27,270.44)	(9.5)
Xerox Corp.	156	508,425.44	414,063.37	(94,362.07)	(18.6)
	2,187	$7,373,504.75	$6,958,221.62	$(415,283.13)	(5.6)%

The results were shocking! Here were the smartest investors in the world and how well did they do? Instead of barely breaking even as in the case of the person who doesn't know any better and just buys and holds, here were the smartest money managers in the world as a group losing an average of 5.6 percent on each trade they made in a group of their twenty favorite stocks.

Taking each stock separately, the institutions did worse by their trading in 14 out of 20 cases than by merely buying and holding. The six exceptions were Avon Products, Pfizer, Sears Roebuck, Simplicity Pattern, Warner Lambert and Xerox. For the most part it was not that they made money in these stocks. They just lost less. For example, while Avon Products dropped 42.8 percent in price, the institutions lost only 13.1 percent. In Pfizer they lost 10.6 percent vs 14.5 percent; Warner Lambert, 9.5 percent vs 11.8 percent and Xerox 18.6 percent vs 44.3 percent. Only in Sears Roebuck and Simplicity Pattern did they manage as a group to both make money and outperform the price action of the stock during this extended review period. In Sears they showed a gain of 12.3 percent vs a gain of only 1.9 percent from $68 to $69 while in Simplicity they eaked out a profit of six tenths of one percent as the stock declined from 27 3/4 to 15 5/8.

Having done this, we next wanted to see how someone following the Low Risk Method might have fared investing in these same 20 stocks during this same period of time. Would they have done better? Or would they have done worse than the most sophisticated professional investors in the nation?

Although it was a lot of work, the test was worth every hour of the time we spent because instead of losing money we found that the use of the Low-Risk Method as described in this book would have shown an investor an average profit of 13.3 percent on each trade during the same 7-year period assuming he bought 100 shares of every stock every time a low risk buy signal was flashed and sold every time a sell signal was recorded. Furthermore each and every stock but one was profitable on balance for the seven years of the test. The exception was Pfizer which showed a loss of 3⅝ points.

To achieve these results an investor using the Low Risk Method would have had to make 105 purchases or an average of 5.25 purchases in each stock over the seven years. Of these, 55 were closed out at a profit and 50 at a loss. A summary of the results is shown on the (right). Not only is this a tremendous improvement over the performance of the institutions but it points out one other important factor: A person can be wrong four or five times out of ten and still do exceedingly well if he keeps his losses small.

Now the test needs to be taken one step further. We need see how an investor would have done under the simulated conditions of running a real portfolio in competition with the best professional investors in the world during this same period of time.

For this, let us assume the 20 institutional favorites make up our complete Master Investment List. Furthermore let's assume we are going to start our investment program with $10,000 which will be

Twenty Institutional Favorite Stocks
Results of Low-Risk Method Signals
January 1, 1970 through December 31, 1976

	# of Trades	Sum of Buys	Sum of Sales	Total Profit	%
American Home Products	7	$377¾	$417½	$39¾	10.5%
AMP Inc.	5	219⅜	298—	78⅝	35.8
Avon Products	4	253⅞	316⅜	62½	24.6
Coca Cola	5	470⅜	520⅞	50½	10.7
Dr. Pepper	5	110⅛	134⅞	24¾	22,5
Dun & Bradstreet	4	182⅛	196¼	14⅛	7.8
Eastman Kodak	3	267¾	341—	73¼	27.4
IBM Corp.	4	1463½	1581¼	117¾	8.0
Int'l Flavors & Frag.	7	341⅞	511⅝	169¾	49.7
Johnson & Johnson	5	554¼	589⅜	35⅛	6.3
Lubrizol Corp.	5	239½	262⅜	22⅞	9.6
Merck & Co.	4	310⅜	401—	90⅝	29.2
Minn. Mining & Mfg.	6	497—	541¾	44¾	9.0
Pfizer	7	210⅛	206½	(3⅝)	(1.7)
Proctor & Gamble	6	545⅛	562⅛	17—	3.1
Schering - Plough	6	372⅞	440⅛	67¼	18.0
Sears Roebuck	5	364⅝	391½	26⅞	7.4
Simplicity Pattern	5	213⅜	259¾	46⅜	21.7
Warner Lambert	5	244¼	275—	30¾	12.6
Xerox Corp.	6	571⅜	603⅞	32½	5.7
Total	104	$7809⅝	$8851⅛	$1041½	13.3%

divided into five equal parts and that we will invest in no more than five different stocks at any one time.

Our test will begin on January 1, 1970. On that date the 15-week advance-decline line is dropping as you can see on page 83. We have already been told that the rule under these circumstances is to defer all purchases. Consequently buying was deferred until July 24 when the 5-week DJI moving average rose above the 15-week average for the first time. A review of the Master Investment list on that date showed there were no stocks meeting our principal buying criteria on such an occasion. That is there were no stocks whose 15-week moving averages were above their 40-week averages. A second look showed only one stock, Dr. Pepper, which met our secondary buying criteria where the 5-week average was above the 40-week average for the first time. Therefore Dr. Pepper was the first stock we purchased. With $2,000 to invest in each of the five stocks it was possible to buy 106 shares of Dr. Pepper on July 24 at about 18¾. In real life of course we probably would have bought just 100 shares but we want to exercise as little discretion in this test as possible.

Week after week the Master Investment List was searched for

additional stocks to buy but none meet the Low-Risk criteria until September 11 when a buy signal was flashed in Sears Roebuck at 65⅞. The following week there were two more buy signals: Johnson & Johnson at 52¾ and Proctor & Gamble at 54. On September 25 we received our fifth buy signal in Simplicity Pattern at 81. With these five signals our portfolio was complete and looked as follows:

Date	Shares Bought	Stock	Price	Debit
7/24/70	106	Dr. Pepper	18¾	$1,987.50
9/11/70	30	Sears Roebuck	65⅞	1,976.25
9/18/70	38	Johnson & Johnson	52¾	2,004.50
9/18/70	37	Proctor & Gamble	54	1,998.00
9/25/70	25	Simplicity Pattern	81	2,025.00
			Unused Credit Balance	$ 8.75

The purchases were well timed because the market continued to advance through the rest of 1970 and well into 1971. Finally, on September 17, 1971 a bear market sell signal was posted. Throughout this entire period our portfolio continued to perform well. It gave no action signals until September 17 when simultaneously with the bear market sell signal, a signal to sell Johnson & Johnson was flashed. Nothing else happened until November 12 when Sears Roebuck is sold and November 19 when Dr. Pepper is sold. We received the following prices on these sales:

Date	Shares Sold	Stock	Price	Credit
		Unused Credit Balance		$ 8.75
9/17/71	38	Johnson & Johnson	90½	$3,439.00
11/12/71	30	Sears Roebuck	91	2,730.00
11/19/71	106	Dr. Pepper	32	3,392.00
				$9,569.75

The three stocks were sold at a profit of $3,592.75 and released almost $9,600 for purchases the next time a new buy signal came along. This occurred on December 31, 1971 at which time eleven of the 20 stocks in the Master List gave buy signals on the same day.

Because this experiment was designed to be as automatic as possible, we decided to buy only the first three stocks, in alphabetical order. These were American Home Products, A.M.P. and Avon Products. Since there was now $9,569.75 in the account, it was possible to buy $3,200 worth of each of these stocks.

Date	Shares Bought	Stock	Price	Debit
12/31/71	36	Amer. Home Products	89⅜	$3,217.50
12/31/71	45	A.M.P., Inc.	71½	3,217.50
12/31/71	31	Avon Products	100⅜	3,111.63
		Unused Credit Balance		$23.12

The next thing we did occurred on July 28, 1972 when we sold Simplicity Pattern which in the interim had been split three for one. Simplicity was sold at 45¼ for a profit of $1,368.75. Then a few months later, on November 24, it was repurchased on another buy signal at 49¾.

The next general sell signal came on April 20, 1973 at which time American Home Products, Avon, and Simplicity Pattern were sold. On May 18, Proctor and Gamble registered its sell signal leaving only A.M.P. to be carried. All the stocks up to this point, including A.M.P. when it was eventually sold on November 23, 1973, were closed out at a profit. These profits ranged from $1,688.22 down to as little as $8.50 but nevertheless, large or small, each trade showed a profit.

Then, in 1973, for some strange reason, the Low-Risk Method went haywire. It failed to work. Five purchases were made between August 3 and October 26 and all five resulted in losses when they were sold out. These losses ranged between $217.00 and $510.00, totaling $2,053.25. Actually, there were twelve buy signals rendered during 1973 by the 20 stocks on the Master Investment List and all lost money on the sale.

The lesson to be learned from this is that every method of investing, no matter how good it is, will not work sometime. Usually it fails to work the first time you try to use it just to test your confidence. Losses, or mistakes, are inevitable, in the entire life process. The thing to remember, however, is that if the procedure you are following is a good one, your losses will be small and the period of time during which your procedure fails to work will be brief.

During 1974 a sprinkling of buy signals were generated but fortunately both the advance-decline line and the Dow Jones Industrial Average was heading down every time a buy signal occurred. This prevented us from buying anything which would later have proved unprofitable.

Finally, in January 1975, the market once more turned up causing us to buy Lubrizol and Warner Lambert in January. Then in February we purchased Dun & Bradstreet, Avon Products, and Proctor and Gamble.

Of these, all but Dun and Bradstreet were sold between July and October. They were replaced by Coca Cola, Eastman Kodak, I.B.M., and Johnson & Johnson on December 26, 1975.

On May 7, 1976 when the market turned uncertain, Coke, D & B, Kodak and Johnson & Johnson were sold for a small profit of $531.25.

Then in response to a buy signal on July 16, 1976, International Flavors was sold to be replaced on September 3 by American Home Products.

We began to close our test on October 8 by selling Lubrizol and Proctor & Gamble on a Low Risk sell signal as the 15 week advance-decline line turned down. American Home Products was sold on October 15 when the Dow Jones Industrial Average confirmed the uncertain market. Then, with the confirmation of a new bear market signal on October 22, I.B.M. was sold, to be followed on November 12 by the sale of Pfizer.

Again in 1976 the results were disappointing until one understands that the overall market did virtually nothing all year as it stayed for the most part in a narrow trading range of only 60 Dow points. The Low Risk Method reflected this by churning out of its December 1975 holdings in May, then flashing what proved to be a false new buy signal just two months later. Like 1973 all purchases made in 1976 were subsequently closed out at losses but the losses were small. And if the bear market signalled late in 1976 turns into another tragedy, the investor using the Low Risk Method will have once again preserved his capital from the onslaught of the Bear.

Remember, the Low Risk Method does not guarantee that you will always make money in the stock market. However, if you choose to invest in a stock that subsequently enjoys a large run up in price, if you buy the stock at the time of a Low Risk buy signal, if you hold it until you get a Low Risk sell signal and if you then sell promptly, you will assure yourself a major portion of the potential profit available from the move. If on the other hand, the stock you choose fails to move, your losses, if you take them promptly should be small. So you see the secret of Low Risk investing, as we will discover in subsequent chapters lies in equal measure with the Low Risk Method and with the idiosyncracities of your own personality. If you have it all together, you will be successful. If you don't, then you have another problem that unfortunately is beyond the scope of this book.

Even with with the small losses of 1973 and 1976 the results of Low Risk investing were excellent. If you care to challenge this, just look over your own confirmation slips for this same period of time. If you did any better, you should be writing, not reading books of this sort because if you look back you will see that from its high in 1973 to its low in 1974, the average stock fell 50 percent while many fell as much

Twenty Institutional Favorite Stocks
Results of Low-Risk Method Signals
Applied to Hypothetical Portfolio
January 1, 1970 — December 31, 1976

	Date	Price	Shares	Buy	Price Sell	Profit	Loss
Dr. Pepper	7-24-70	18¾	106	$1987.50			
Sears Roebuck	9-11-70	65⅞	30	1976.25			
Johnson & Johnson	9-18-70	52¾	38	2004.50			
Proctor & Gamble	9-25-70	54	37	1998.00			
Simplicity Pattern	9-25-70	81	25	2025.00			
Johnson & Johnson	9-17-71	90½	38		3439.00	1434.50	
Sears Roebuck	11-12-71	91	30		2730.00	753.75	
Dr. Pepper	11-19-71	32	106		3392.00	1404.50	
Amer. Home Products	12-31-71	89⅜	36	3217.50			
AMP Inc.	12-31-71	71½	45	3217.50			
Avon Products	12-31-71	100⅜	31	3111.63			
Simplicity Pattern	7-28-72	45¼	75		3393.75	1368.75	
Simplicity Pattern	11-24-72	49¾	68	3383.00			
Amer. Home Products	4-20-73	126½	36		4554.00	1336.50	
Avon Products	4-20-73	132¾	31		4115.25	1003.62	
Simplicity Pattern	4-20-73	49⅞	68		3391.50	8.50	
Proctor & Gamble	5-18-73	99⅝	37		3686.12	1688.12	
Amer. Home Products	8- 3-73	45⅞	85	3899.38			
Pfizer & Co.	8- 3-73	49⅛	80	3930.00			
Proctor & Gamble	8- 3-73	112¾	35	3946.25			
Simplicity Pattern	8- 3-73	53½	74	3959.00			
Proctor & Gamble	8-31-73	98½	35		3447.50		498.75
Johnson & Johnson	10-26-73	123¼	28	3451.00			
Amer. Home Products	11-23-73	42⅛	85		3580.62		318.76
AMP Inc.	11-23-73	45¾	135		6095.59	2878.09	
Simplicity Pattern	11-23-73	46⅝	74		3450.25		508.75
Pfizer & Co.	11-30-73	42¾	80		3420.00		510.00
Johnson & Johnson	12- 7-73	115½	28		3234.00		217.00
Lubrizol	1-10-75	37⅝	105	3950.63			
Warner Lambert	1-17-75	25⅞	153	3958.88			
Dun & Bradstreet	2- 7-75	23¾	167	3966.25			
Avon Products	2-14-75	36⅜	110	3973.75			
Proctor & Gamble	2-14-75	96¼	41	3946.25			
Proctor & Gamble	7-11-75	96¼	41		3946.25		
Warner Lambert	8- 1-75	33	153		5049.00	1090.12	
Avon Products	10-17-75	40⅞	110		4496.25	522.50	
Lubrizol	10-17-75	46¼	105		4856.25	905.62	
Coca Cola	12-26-75	83¾	54	4522.50			
Eastman Kodak	12-26-75	108⅛	42	4541.25			
IBM	12-26-75	223¼	21	4688.25			
Johnson & Johnson	12-26-75	90½	51	4615.50			
Coca Cola	5- 7-76	85	54		4590.00	67.50	
Dun & Bradstreet	5- 7-76	28⅛	167		4696.88	730.63	
Eastman Kodak	5- 7-76	105¾	42		4420.50		120.75

	Date	Price	Shares	Buy	Price Sell	Profit	Loss
Johnson & Johnson	5- 7-76	87¾	51		4475.25		140.25
Int'l Flavors & Frag	7-16-76	25⅞	175	4528.12			
Lubrizol	7-16-76	41½	109	4523.50			
Pfizer & Co.	7-16-76	29⅛	155	4514.38			
Proctor & Gamble	7-16-76	97¾	45	4398.75			
Int'l Flavors & Frag	8- 6-76	25½	175		4462.50		65.62
Amer. Home Products	9- 3-76	34⅜	133	4571.88			
Lubrizol	10- 8-76	37½	109		4087.50		436.00
Proctor & Gamble	10- 8-76	93¼	45		4196.25		202.50
Amer. Home Products	10-15-76	32⅞	133		4372.38		199.50
IBM	10-22-76	256½	21		5386.50	698.25	
Pfizer & Co.	11-12-76	26⅜	155		4088.13		426.25
Totals				$102,806.40	$115,053.22	$15,890.95	$3,644.13
Net Profit						$12,246.82	

as 80 to 90 percent. This was the most vicious bear market since the Great Crash of 1929. As a consequence, the life savings of hundreds of thousands of Americans evaporated into thin air.

Nevertheless a test on the above portfolio arbitrarily chosen from among many that are constantly being circulated reveals that it is not only possible to keep your estate intact during times of trouble but actually make it grow at the same time. During our test, the savings we started with actually increased over 122 percent!

This was accomplished in spite of the fact that there were almost as many unprofitable investments as there were winners. Actually, of 28 completed trades, only 15 were profitable while 12 were losers and one a draw. The secret was that the profits were allowed to ride and were therefore much larger than the losses. The average profit was $1,059.40 while the average loss was only $303.68. If the Low Risk Method works this well during a period of great disaster, think how well it is likely to perform the next time we get a genuine super bull market.

There are several morals to this story. One is that you can't win all the time and you don't have to. You can lose almost half of the time and still come out ahead if you keep your profits small and let your profits run. The second moral is that you don't have to worry about the pros in the big Institutions. Once you learn the principles in this book you can do as well as they do.

Before we move on, here is a comparison of how well the different tests described in this chapter turned out. Since the numbers are not comparable, the key to the comparisons are the percentages.

1. Here we bought one share of each of the 20 stocks on January 1, 1970 and sold them on December 31, 1976.

The total value of the purchases was	$1,194.50
The total value of the sales was	$1,201.25
This resulted in a profit of	$ 6.75
Which as a percent comes to	0.6%

2. This shows the actual, on-balance performance results of the 2,000 largest institutional investors in these same stocks for the same period of time.

Their purchases were worth (000 omitted)	$7,373,505
Their sales amounted to	$6,958,222
Giving them a loss of	$ (415,283)
As a percent this comes to	(5.1)%

3. Compared to the above, the theoretical performance of our Low Risk Method taking into account all the signals and assuming the purchase or sale of one share of stock on each signal gave us the following:

The total of the purchases amounted to	$7,809.63
The sales netted us	$8,851.13
Giving us a profit of	$1,041.50
Which as a percentage comes to	13.3%

4. Finally, by taking the buy and sell signals generated in example #3 above and using them to make investments according to the rules described in this book,

We started with an initial investment of	$10,000.00
Which at the end of the test had grown to	$22,246.82
Giving us a profit of	$12,246.82
Or a percent profit for 7 years of	124.5%

In summary, while the typical experience of the average investor was that he either lost his shirt or at best broke even during this test period which saw some of the worst bear markets in history, it was possible for the Low Risk Investor not only to survive, but to more than double the monetary value of his portfolio.

35 Review of Investment Strategy

FUNDAMENTALS There is often no correlation between the price of a stock and the fundamentals relating to the company represented by that stock. Fundamentals do, however, determine in a general way whether or not investors are likely to be attracted to or repulsed from a stock.

BULL-AND-BEAR MARKETS The market moves regularly from a period of bull-market conditions to one of bear-market conditions. In recent years, the bottoms of each bear market have been from three and a half to four and a half years removed from one bear-market bottom to the next. This has been true regardless of the economic conditions prevailing at the time.

INVESTOR PSYCHOLOGY The switch, from bear market to bull market and back again, is not the result of economic conditions, therefore, but is due instead to a regular switch of investor psychology from optimism to pessimism. These changes in investor attitudes trigger the kind of actions that make prices rise when more and more investors become optimistic and then cause prices to drop as investors become depressed and then panic.

HERD ACTION OF STOCKS Stocks do not go up and down in a random fashion. Instead they have a tendency to go up and down together during bull-and-bear markets, with just enough exceptions to prove the rule. Therefore, most investors will do as well or better if they know *when* to buy a representative selection of stocks instead of spending too much time and effort in a quest for the one stock that will go up regardless of the trend.

SHOPPING LIST A shopping list of representative stocks that the investor would be willing to own, providing the time is right, should be prepared and maintained. This shopping list should include:

1. A limited number of no less than 25 and no more than 100,
2. Cyclical stocks that historically fluctuate widely between their bull-market highs and bear-market lows; and
3. Growth stocks that have tripped temporarily during the most recent bear market but whose operating records continue to improve.

MARKET INDICATORS Only the market itself can tell you what to do. Everything else is irrelevant. While the irrelevant items tell you what the market ought to be doing, this may or may not be what it actually is doing. You can determine what the market is doing if each week you will compute:

1. The 5-week moving-average price of the Dow Jones Industrial average and that of each stock in your shopping list;
2. The 15-week moving averages of these same items;
3. Their 40-week moving averages;
4. The 15-week moving average of the weekly cumulative total of stocks advancing minus those declining.

TIMING THE MARKET The primary trend of the market tells you when to buy stocks and when to avoid buying stocks. It does not tell you when to sell them. Once stocks have been purchased, their trend action tells you when to sell them. The following guide to the primary trend of the market should be kept in mind.

There are four basic market conditions:

1. A bull market.
2. An uncertain period within a bull market. This is a period when prices drop and investors begin to fear that the bull market is finished. Most uncertain periods in bull markets resolve themselves when prices drop low enough to give investors a second opportunity to buy stocks at bargain prices. Most investors however are too frightened at such times to take advantage of these bargains.

Eventually one of these bull market reactions is of such duration that in retrospect it is seen as the first decline in a new bear market.

3. A bear market.
4. An uncertain period in a continuing bear market. This is a period when the market starts to rally. Most bear market rallys resolve themselves by fizzling out just as large numbers of investors begin to convince themselves that a new bull market has started. As a result they buy more stock instead of using this as an opportunity either to lighten up their holdings or to sell stock short.

Eventually one of these rallys is so strong that it turns the market around and is seen in retrospect as the first rally of a new bull market.

The proper investment stance to take with respect to the market and to individual stocks under the above market conditions is summarized in the accompanying schedules.

In them, the terms + or −40 mean that the average price is either above (+) or below (−) that of the 40-week average price. UP means that the moving average in question is registering a higher value each successive week. DOWN indicates that it is registering successive lower numbers.

DJI Moving Average			A-D Line	
5-week	15-week	40-week	15-week	Investment Posture
−40	−40	DOWN	DOWN	Bear Market (Avoid new purchases)
−40	−40	UP	DOWN	Ditto
UP/−40	−40	DOWN	DOWN	Uncertain (Probably rally in bear market)
+40	−40	DOWN	DOWN	Uncertain (Possibly first sign of new bull market-B
−40	−40	DOWN	UP	Ditto
+40	−40	DOWN	UP	Second sign of a new bull market-BUY
+40	+40	DOWN	UP	Buy aggressively-or stay invested-Bull Market
+40	+40	UP	UP	Bull market (Stay fully invested)
−40	+40	UP	UP	Uncertain (Stay invested but do not make new purchases)
+40	+40	UP	DOWN	Ditto
+/−40	−40	UP	UP	Bear Market
+/−40	−40	UP	DOWN	Bear Market

TIMING INDIVIDUAL STOCKS The primary trend of each stock in your Master Investment List tells you what your investment posture should be. Here is a summary of the various investment posture combinations for individual stocks:

Individual Moving Average			
5-week	15-week	40-week	Investment Posture
+40	+40	UP	Hold, if owned, regardless of general market
+40	+40	DOWN	Ditto
−15	+40	UP	Hold if bull market - sell if bear market
−15	+40	DOWN	Ditto
−40	+40	UP	Ditto
−40	+40	DOWN	Ditto
+40	−40	UP	Buy in early stages of bull markets - Avoid in bear markets
+40	−40	DOWN	Ditto
−40	−40	UP/DOWN	Avoid regardless of general market

PART VII

What Makes You, You

36. The Keys to Investment Success

The techniques we have just studied constitute all that an investor really has to know to achieve consistently profitable stock-market results. Over the years, any investor who each week performs the mathematical computations recommended in this book, and then relies on them to buy and sell when signaled to do so, will find himself in that small minority banking large and consistent stock-market profits.

Any losses he will have—and there will be some, as our examples illustrated—will be strictly limited, but the profit potential in some cases will be almost limitless. An after-tax return of more than 25 percent per year in a representative portfolio of investments is a reasonable expectancy; a return greatly in excess of that amount is a distinct possibility. All that is necessary to achieve these results is the willingness to spend several hours each week making a few basic calculations, and to ignore virtually everything else that is supposed to affect the market.

The stock market is really this simple!

This is all there is to raking down consistently large stock-market profits. Yet, sad to say, no investor past, present, and future can ever completely realize the full potential of this system and what the stock market has to offer him. The reasons for this do not rest in the stock market or the system but in the investor himself. As we observed in the introduction to this book, it is probable that as many as 80 percent of all investors not only fail to achieve any investment success but instead consistently lose money in the process.

When you understand why, you have found the second key to investment success. The investment method you have just learned is the first key, the key to Low-Risk Investing. This methodology puts at the investor's command specific guidelines that will tell him at any given moment just what his investment posture should be, not only with respect to the general market but with respect to any specific stock he may wish to follow. This is the easy part of the investment process.

The second key is much harder to obtain because it carries with it a price that, while not high, is much more than most people seem willing to pay—the willingness of each investor to come to grips with himself, with the real person behind the man he pretends to be. It involves a desire, in the language of the philosophers over the years, to "know thyself" and your relationship to others, and to study your own strengths and weaknesses in your emotional response to the action of stocks. This difference in individual reactions to external events is, more than any other influence, directly responsible for causing many people to rush and sell their stocks in panic at stock-market bottoms while others, on the other hand, observing the same events will calmly and coolly buy up all the stock that is offered.

At first glance, this would not appear to have anything to do with the question of investment success, but as we go on from here, you will see that it has almost everything to do with it. The discipline an investor develops as he comes to grip with his own nature allows him to follow a rationally profitable course of stock-market action. When an investor acts from a base of knowledge, he can hold in check the unconscious emotional triggers that often compel him to do the things that lead to his selling out at market bottoms and buying back in again at market tops.

37. Do You Really Want to Make Stock-Market Profits?

Now that the investor is aware of the Low-Risk Method of Successful Investing, he must decide once and for all whether he really wants to be one of the minority of successful investors.

This is important because, despite appearances to the contrary, each investor is individually the sole determinate of whether or not he is going to be a successful investor. In other words, the odds for or against success are individually determined. No one can make an investor successful if he does not want to be successful. This type of investor would find some way to frustrate all the wise counsel given him. On the other hand, no one can keep success away from an investor once he is determined to succeed.

Numerous examples abound of people who started with virtually nothing and accumulated great wealth in the market. It can be mathematically demonstrated that a thousand-dollar investment can grow to a million dollars in less than twenty years, provided that after-tax capital gains can grow at the rate of 50 percent per year. The Brunswick and Boeing illustrations show that gains of such magnitude, while not always certain, are at least not out of reach.

Nevertheless, just as many examples exist of people who were wiped out by the market. Many psychologists contend that investors use the market as a means of deliberately punishing themselves. Some people don't really expect and many don't really want to be successful. Whether they realize it or not, the way they approach the market shouts to the world their desire to lose.

Investors who want to lose treat the market like a gambling casino where they know in advance the odds are fixed against them. Then they play at the game of investing in a way that will justify their anticipations. They never even want to consider that *in the stock market each man sets his own odds,* and aggressively fight off every attempt to bring order and profit into their investment experience.

Still other investors put unrealistic demands on the market in terms of anticipated returns versus the time of unfoldment. Often it is not that their hoped-for return is unrealistic so much as the stock they buy is not suitable for the *time* these investors choose to come into the market. Their investments are made out of desperation and pressure; the results they get are the results of this desperation and pressure.

Therefore, after evolving a *modus operandi* such as the Low-Risk Method, the next step to success is either the simplest or the most difficult one in the process. It involves a willingness to let the market tell *you* what to do and when to do it rather than the other way around, and a belief that the method you are using will in the long run be successful despite occasional setbacks.

38. Accept Full Responsibility for Your Investment Decisions

The next hurdle the investor must face is the question of whether or not he is mature enough to take full responsibility for his stock-market actions.

So often you hear an investor say, "That damned broker of mine. When I buy stocks myself, I do alright. But every time I listen to him I lose money." It is inconceivable that the first Rockefeller or Edison, Ford or Rothschild, or any other successful or wealthy person past, present, or future ever became wealthy by abdicating his decision-making authority to someone else. All successful people have advisers and they look for the best ones they can get. Many of them in fact delegate quite a bit of authority to their advisers because they trust them and know their judgment is good. But when it comes to making the final decisions, they always reserve the right to veto the decisions of their advisers and to change advisers when necessary.

It is hard to believe that any investor with knowledge of the Low-Risk Method of Successful Investing, would ever dream of asking his broker for advice. About the only counsel a broker could give him would be to point out attractive new stocks to include in a master selection list. Nevertheless, many investors lack confidence in themselves and permit their brokers to make investment decisions for them. No broker, under any circumstances should be given carte-blanche authority to make all such decisions without the investor reserving for himself the right to override the broker's decisions.

An investor who cannot or will not make his own investment decisions should either stay out of the market or be willing to pay an adviser to manage his account for him. Even this involves decision making on the part of the investor. First, he has to know enough to pick a good adviser. Secondly, he has to know enough to recognize unsatisfactory advice and have the fortitude to fire that adviser. The investor who is neither willing to make his own decisions nor pay a competent person to make them for him deserves the quality of performance he gets.

The successful investor then is not merely the man who is confident of his success, but if the situation requires, he is also capable of choosing competent consultants. Beyond this, he is willing to accept responsibility for his blunders as well as his correct decisions without blaming others. When it comes to investment success, it cannot be any other way.

39. It's Your Money—Spend Some Time Making It Work For You

Most people work pretty hard to earn their daily bread, either mentally, physically, or in the frustration they generate on a job they can't stand. They do all this in order to make a living at something that for many is no fun. To try to get off this treadmill, to break away from the rat race, many people turn to Wall Street whenever they get a few extra dollars in an effort to compound them. They look on Wall Street as an easy road to instant riches. Here is where their common sense breaks down.

While most people are willing to go to almost any extreme to systematically allocate their resources of time and effort to accumulate a nest egg, most of these same people seem unwilling when they become investors to make any effort to sensibly direct their efforts and money on Wall Street.

It is appalling to see how many people will, without a moment's hesitation, put all their hard-earned cash into a stock that they know absolutely nothing about. A surprisingly large number of people seem willing to invest in anything from a sixty-second recommendation from a broker they may not even know to an out-of-context fragment of a conversation overheard on a train, in a restaurant, or in a bar. Very few people are willing to go about the business of investing on an organized, calculated basis; to invest a few minutes or hours of their time each week working at their investments in the way the Low-Risk Method demands. In this respect alone, Low-Risk investors have an incalculable advantage over at least 90 percent of their fellow investors.

Inordinately large sums of money are invested on the basis of surprisingly superficial efforts. For brief periods of time, these superficial approaches to investing sometimes seem to work. During some bull markets anything works. It is only when the trend turns and these casual investors are stuck with large losses in their stocks that they seem genuinely shocked, hurt, and indignant to learn that they have nothing to shown for their foray into the market but a tax loss on their tax return.

Even when investors do investigate before proceeding, they often don't do much better because their explorations are focused on irrelevancies. They investigate stocks on the basis of factors that ought to make the stocks go up or down, not on the basis of those that are making a stock go up or down at that moment.

They compound their problem with an abominable sense of timing. Most people buy stocks when they have the money to buy them. This is a self-evident truism but the flaw in the truism is that when most people have money to invest in stocks, most stocks are priced so high that they do not represent sound, Low-Risk investment values.

When an investor has money to invest, chances are so does his neighbor. About the time everyone has managed to save enough to think about investing and feel confident that their personal financial problems are under control, everyone else around them probably has the same idea. They all have seen how much stocks have moved up in price since the end of the last bear market and they all want to get in on a good thing. There is just one thing wrong. They are all too late!

On the other hand, few people have money to invest when the country is in the middle of a recession. At these times many people are unemployed, many of those who are working are not getting the overtime pay they were used to during boom periods, and others are making just enough to meet their monthly expenses. During times like these, even people who do have money saved and available for investment are reluctant to do so. They see the financial problems their neighbors are having and are afraid the same thing might happen to them.

This is what makes even good stocks underpriced during bear markets. It's simply a combination of people who must sell stocks on one hand and people who are afraid to buy stocks on the other.

Somehow, the investor who wants to make the profits Wall Street can provide him must break himself away from this self-destructive circle. He has to go about the business of investing backward.

As he saves his money, he has to train himself to put it in a savings bank and wait for the next substantial drop in prices. Unlike the average investor, the successful investor does not doubt that the market will never go down again. He knows that it always has and that it always will, just as regular as clockwork.

He knows that when everyone has money to put into the stock market, there is too much competition for stock because the supply is limited. When that happens, prices go up. Then, when everyone has spent their money buying stocks, prices start to drift off. When this happens, it scares some people half to death, causing them to sell and make prices fall even more. This gets prices down to where they are bargains, but instead of buying stocks at this point, the same people who rushed to buy stocks when prices were high now seem to panic and rush to sell at the worst time and prices possible.

That is why the small group of Low-Risk investors who wait patiently are able to buy all their stocks at such low end-of-season, clearance-sale, distress prices. They don't need to do anything to force investors to sell at the bottom because most people do it to themselves.

The Low-Risk Method of Investment Success helps an investor get in step with these successful investors. Just at the time his unsuccessful neighbors will be most intent on buying stocks, his Master List will show him that the price performance of more and more stocks is such that they should be sold. Like the successful investors, he, too, will become cautious in the face of such exuberance. Then, when all his neighbors are in a state of panic, his Master List will show the strongest stocks, one after the other, turning around to begin their new bull markets. This will give him courage and confidence to withdraw his money from the bank and buy stocks at bargain levels.

With respect to his investments, the investor should never forget that it is his money that is riding on the line. He acquired it in one way or another, and if it was worth making and saving in the first place, it has to be worth the effort to hold on to and make grow intelligently.

An investor shouldn't go into the market as though he didn't give a damn about what happens to his money once he invests it. If he doesn't exhibit the necessary caution and self-control to conserve and increase his assets intelligently, it is ludicrous to expect anyone else will go out of their way to exercise these restraints for him.

40. Investors Are Human

The biggest stumbling block to successful investing is simply that you and I, along with our 30 million fellow investors, are human beings. This is what the stock market is all about. It is nothing more than people acting like people and doing all the dumb, stupid things people so often do.

The only way to become a successful investor is to first learn how you and others behave and to then find a way to divorce yourself from your more irrational patterns of behavior. The successful investor is usually the one who has found some way of becoming detached from himself and from the market. He has learned to make his decisions automatically, instinctively, logically, and without much apparent thought or effort, more like a machine than a human being.

This is why the Low-Risk Method is so valuable. Regularly, once each week, it gives the investor a precise, unequivocal investment decision with respect to each stock he follows. On occasion that decision is incorrect but it is never uncertain. It never leaves the investor confused as to what action to take.

A major difficulty of investors stems from the expectation that tomorrow is going to be just like today. If today were a good day, it's going to be like this forever. If today was rotten, we fall apart and despair. We don't think that things will ever get better again. People seldom seem to adjust for the probability—in fact, the certainty—of change, yet the story of the stock market is one of constant change. In the stock market, things are never what they are today. Tomorrow they may be better or they may be worse, but they are seldom just the same.

The stock market holds an unbelievably enormous potential in store for investors alert to seize this potential. But because investors do not allow for change, they very seldom see opportunity at the beginning nor can they visualize the dangers at the end of market moves.

Unfortunately, market moves seem clear only when looking back in retrospect. In retrospect, everything is self-evident. But now, with the Low-Risk Method of Successful Investing, even the future can become at least partially self-evident. Stock-market profits will become easier to achieve once the investor gets into the habit of responding instinctively to the Low-Risk signals flashed by his computations. With respect to his performance in the stock market, he will become something akin to the well-trained, champion athlete who learns to respond instinctively to the demands of his sport.

At the same time the investor must understand that he is still human and therefore susceptible to occasional mistakes. These mistakes will cost him money but, as the Brunswick example illustrated, the extent of his losses should be limited. Overriding concern with infallibility is counterproductive to investment success. People overly concerned with perfection tend to worry too much. When they worry, they not only lose their confidence but they also become extremely tense. They lose their ability to think clearly and to measure alternative courses of action properly.

Because of the human element involved in investing, successful investing continues to be as much of an art as it is a science, regardless of how precise systems such as the Low-Risk Method attempt to be. A successful investor, therefore, is an artist. Like all thriving artists, the investor eventually comes to recognize that many of his successful investments—his masterpieces, if you will—are the result of a combination of knowing how to properly interpret the market and some kind of human intuitive process that he senses at work in him but which he cannot adequately explain to anyone else.

41. Investors Need to Disagree

The investor should also be aware of one of the basic paradoxes about the stock market. The paradox is that, for the market to function effectively, there have to be two participants for each and every transaction; and that each of these participants has to be in basic disagreement with the other as to the future direction the stock they are interested in is going to take. Every time we all agree as to the course of the market, it breaks down because there is no one to trade with; there is no one to take the other side.

On the other hand, every time there is a basic disagreement as to the future course of the market, the market functions beautifully and large quantities of stock often trade at very small changes in price. As a result, for you to be right all the time, others would have to be wrong all the time, and in the greater scheme of things this would be bad for both of you. Therefore, what is more likely is that you will be only partially right only part of the time and so will the other fellow. This is highlighted in the Low-Risk Method in that it is not designed to catch the tops or bottoms of major market movements. Instead, the Low-Risk investor is content to merely buy and sell soon after major market movements change direction.

The stock market could not accommodate all investors if they were right all the time, because in essence the stock market is nothing more and nothing less than an auction place. In that sense, it is designed to resolve the simultaneous differences of opinion that occur because someone has reached a decision to buy a stock at the same time someone else has reached a decision to sell that same stock. Then they both go one step further and transform that decision into an actual order to buy or sell that stock.

Then, and only then, is it possible to have an effectively functioning market place. It is not only desirable but absolutely imperative that every time you decide to buy or sell a stock, there is someone available who disagrees with you to the point where he is willing to do the exact opposite.

When the collective judgment of investors is such that they all agree, then the market breaks down. When everyone wants to sell, you have the bear markets that most people fear so much. In the greater sense, however, they create the beautiful buying opportunities that are spawned out of such panic.

Alternatively, when everyone wants to buy and there is no one to sell to them, the stage is set for the very sharp moves up in price that appear so exhilarating for awhile. Actually they serve merely to trap many people into high-cost positions and bring on the inevitable sharp drops in price and investor losses later on.

42. Investors' Emotions Play an Important Part in Their Investment Decisions

A discerning investor eventually discovers that he not only operates in the stock market as a continuously changing and evolving personality, but he also operates within a constantly changing emotional framework. These constantly changing emotions shuttle him back and forth between his own individual parameters of confidence and despair. With many investors, emotions play a bigger part in determining what and when they buy and sell than any discernible intellectual process. This is why they lose money so often.

For anyone to be consistently successful in the stock market, the process has to be reversed. In the stock market, the more often investment decisions are based on logic rather than emotion, the more often they are likely to be profitable.

Imagine, if you can, an emotional scale with irrational ecstacy at one end and abysmal despair at the other. Most people operate within a range of emotions that fit somewhere on this scale. The emotional range of each person is different. The range of emotions some of us experience is rather wide; for others, it is less extreme.

Although every investor must cope with emotions—this is a prerequisite of experiencing life—some are lucky because their emotions generally fall within the optimistic portion of the scale. Many others, unfortunately, operate within the pessimistic half of the scale most of the time.

This emotional outlook is important because investors tend to interpret changes in the market according to their own emotional points of view at the moment. For instance, if an unexpected crisis develops in an investor's stocks while he is in a confident frame of mind, it is easier for him to resolve it favorably than when he is feeling pessimistic. In a state of confidence, the investor is likely to react in such a way that, if he cannot turn the crisis into a personal advantage, at least he can salvage it from becoming a total loss.

It is important that the investor come to grips with, and correctly assess, his particular emotional frame of reference. If he finds he has a generally pessimistic outlook, this may explain—at least partially—why he has continuously found reasons to sell his stocks at precisely the wrong times in the past.

Knowing he has a negative point of view will also enable the investor to correct it if he wants to. What he needs to change in order to make a negative frame of reference a positive one are two things: knowledge and attitude. Dozens, perhaps hundreds, of books have been written about mental attitudes, success habits, and so on, but it has often been difficult to offer definite evidence of the validity of these theories. In the stock market, however, these concepts can be tested and proved by an investor who cares to submit himself to the test.

A pessimistic investor need only work with the Low-Risk techniques described in this book. These techniques will give him knowledge, and with this knowledge he has gained, the confidence to act in accordance. When the techniques signal Low-Risk areas for making purchases, the investor should by then be sufficiently confident to act. If he finds this difficult, he should than attempt to deliberately seek to change his attitude and make some purchases, anyway. As the bull market actually materializes and an investor's profits grow, it should become increasingly easier for him to adopt a positive mental attitude toward investing in the future. In this manner an adverse emotional framework can deliberately be shifted upward into a more optimistic range.

Even though an investor has shifted his emotional framework upward on the scale, he might still experience as wide a range of emotions as before. Now, however, the worst he might experience might be serious concern about a stock that does something unexpected, whereas before he might have gone into a state of panic and despair.

As a result of this increased confidence, he is able to look for and find more profitable investment opportunities than ever before.

43. Investors Are Often Involuntarily Triggered into Taking Action

Another danger all investors face is the prospect of being triggered into buying or selling something involuntarily and that they will come to regret this action.

If, for example, an investor is already in a depressed state of mind, something like this might conceivably occur. Let us say his broker calls him and says that something entirely unexpected and not particularly good has happened to one of the companies whose stock the investor owns. Because this news was unexpected, because it was bad, and because the investor's emotional outlook was pessimistically inclined at the moment, he is likely to act impulsively and order his broker to sell him out.

Later on, when the investor has had an opportunity to digest the news and after the peak of his pessimism has passed, he may decide that the news was not so bad, after all, and he might well have cause to regret the sale of his stock. Because of the danger of such a development, many investors ask their brokers not to call them under any circumstances during trading hours. They prefer to have their brokers call them after the market closes or to read the news in the paper that evening. This gives them time to weigh the alternatives and plan a proper response.

Calm investors who follow the Low-Risk Method will find there are very few surprises, except for the occasional catastrophes of nature that they cannot anticipate. They know that almost everything reflects itself in the changing pattern of prices, and they find themselves well trained to interpret and react to these changing price patterns.

44. It's You Against the World

In its simplest form, the struggle to achieve consistent stock-market profits involves a struggle, an interfacing between two worlds, or universes. One of these universes is you, the individual investor. The other universe is everything else that exists. All the other investors, all the stocks available for you to invest in, all the elements and forces that determine the level at which stock prices are to sell, exclusive of what you yourself do, are in this other universe.

Your success or failure, or the degree of your relative success or failure, is wholly dependent on how successfully your individual universe interfaces with this larger universe. To the extent that you can clearly see what is happening in the stock market and can effectively adapt your own actions to the activity in this larger universe, you will be successful. To the extent that you fail to adapt, you will be relatively less successful.

Within yourself you can control to some degree your emotions, your actions, and your reactions. In the larger universe, you generally have very little voice. You will, for the most part, have very little control over what is happening there. You will generally have very little to say about who your opponents or partners will be; what they will do, when they will do it, and why. In other words, you will generally have very little knowledge about why the market and those who are participating in it are behaving as they do. From where you sit, you will most of the time have only a very limited understanding and viewpoint of what is happening. And yet, on that limited point of view and on that limited understanding, your total success or failure as an investor depends.

It therefore becomes imperative that you see and understand the situation from your restricted perspective as clearly as possible. As we have seen, the poor habit patterns of investors produce a condition akin to mental cataracts or mental astigmatism that obscures their vision. On the other hand, focusing too clearly on something that is extraneous can also lead to erroneous conclusions.

This was the challenge to the Low-Risk Method—to find some way to understand what was happening in that big universe without ignoring the details. We had to find a way to gain sufficient long-term market perspective, using the least number of variables possible, because too much was happening in that big universe for us to know everything.

The combination of factors that finally developed combine the essential aspects of fundamental analysis with the price activity of individual stocks and the action of the market as a whole. This approach permits you to concentrate on those elements necessary for capital accumulation and to ignore all the extraneous factors. It allows each investor who chooses to follow the method to achieve creditable results in the stock market, despite developments in that larger universe over which he has no control.

45. Modern Alchemy

The effort on the part of investors to make money in the stock market today is in many respects like attempts of the alchemists of the Middle Ages to transmute lead into gold. There was a lot of talk then about these people who were supposed to be able to perform this miracle, but no one probably knew anyone who could really do it. It's much the same today. After all the thousands of books that have been written on the stock market, very few of their readers can point to someone they know who actually pyramided a thousand dollars into a million and then succeeded in holding on to his profits.

Alchemists probably never manufactured any gold, but they nevertheless did lay the groundwork for much of today's knowledge in chemistry and physics, including our ability to change the structure of basic chemical compositions into the many useful products in use today.

The alchemist was not able to change lead into gold, but he sometimes achieved something just as important. The discipline and effort that went into his search had the effect of transforming many alchemists into controlled, well-disciplined individuals, able to turn those challenges that face everyone into personal advantage in one way or another.

This is almost exactly the kind of self-discipline that most successful investors bring into the market with them. However poorly disciplined they might be in other areas, the successful investor is well disciplined about those things he needs to know to succeed in the stock market. As we have seen, most investors have little or nothing to show for their efforts at the end of each stock-market cycle. Their lack of discipline causes them to lose money, often big money and sometimes everything they own.

Yet anyone looking at the price range of almost any stock in almost any year can readily see that here, in the spread between their high and low prices, is the potential for unlimited wealth if even a small part of this annual spread could be regularly captured. This is the goal of the modern-day investor. His degree of discipline and knowledge of what to look for together form the catalyst by which he can achieve his goal.

Actually, making money in the stock market is easy. It is so ridiculously easy as to be almost pathetic. But most investors never achieve their goals because something in their personal make-ups that they cannot control keeps tripping them up. These factors, whatever they are, have to be brought under control, have to be "transmuted," in other words, before those stock-market profits available almost for the asking can be tapped.

PART VIII

This
and That

46. Don't Confuse the Issue

The only reason an investor should ever buy a stock is with the idea that he can sell it at some future date at a price higher than he originally paid for it. Everything else is inconsequential. Unless an investor starts with this premise and keeps it firmly in mind, nothing else will turn out right.

Stocks are not bought because of "good fundamentals." Stocks are not avoided because the management is crooked. Stocks are not held or disposed of because the company does or does not perform a social service. All this is irrelevant to the business of investing.

Once the technical position of a stock becomes sufficiently strong and the price trend of a stock is accelerating, the stock may continue to move up regardless of how inept the management is. On the other hand, even the best management would find it impossible to prevent a technically weak stock from falling during a bear market.

The investor should always keep in mind that when the *time* is right, even the shaggiest dog of a stock will outperform the finest blue chips. On the other hand, when the *time* is wrong, even the bluest of blue chips will lose a fortune for its owner.

With this in mind, the investor can keep his perspective and his mind on his objective. He can keep his mind on what stocks *are* doing rather than on what they *ought to be doing*.

When fundamentals, quality of management, social awareness, and other things an investor "ought to know" are relevant to his needs, he should adjust to them. At all other times, he should be aware of such items only as conversational tidbits at cocktail parties, where conversation is largely irrelevant, anyway.

47. Investors' Emotions Are Constantly in a State of Flux

Regardless of whatever happens, the way in which you as an investor will react to an event at one time will be different from how you will react to the same thing at some other time. This is true of individuals and groups.

Therefore, the price level of a stock is not so much a measure of anything related to the value of its company as it is a measure of how excited or depressed, rightly or wrongly, people are about the company and the nation. High stock prices tell those who care to know that people are optimistic and confident about their jobs, their families, their futures. Low stock prices mirror the fears and anxieties of the population.

The ease, therefore, with which stock prices move both up and down as a result of the auction-market process serves as the most sensitive indicator ever developed for measuring the shifting state of mass emotional behavior and for registering the speed with which these shifts sometimes occur.

48. Stock-Market Panics

Stock-market panics occur regularly. Each time the market drops, at the end of the decline a brief period is likely to occur—sometimes lasting only a few hours, sometimes a few days—when a state of panic sets in.

During such times it is important to remember the old adage, "Stock-market panics are not a matter of the purse but of the mind." Excluding the investor who permits himself to be triggered into selling out during the height of the panic, the market generally benefits from market panics. They are healthy because they clear the air of the gloom that has been hanging over the market. They allow the fear and the other negative emotions that accompanied the decline to dissipate, much like the way a bolt of lightning discharges the accumulated static electricity from a cloud. Stock-market panics help bring back a state of balance to a market situation that was previously imbalanced. They usually do not last long, and when they are over, prices often recover quickly. Except for the person who was triggered into selling, it is almost as though there had never been anything to worry about.

The Low-Risk Method anticipates the major declines that can lead to serious panics and helps investors withdraw from the market well before panic phases set in. Low-Risk investing anticipates panics from two points of view: first, as something not to get involved in as they are evolving; then, as something to look forward to as a period of recurring opportunity.

During bear markets, disillusioned investors and their legislators look for ways to legislate falling prices out of existence, but they are unwilling at the same time to rule against the rise of stocks in the first place. They will never succeed because rising and falling prices are but two sides of the same coin. As a mechanism for the instant adjustment of buying and selling imbalances, a changing price level is as normal and rational as the process of breathing.

49. The Investor-Market Relationship

The fact that stock prices move up and down is neither good nor bad in and of itself. What is important is how the investor reacts and adjusts himself to these constantly changing price levels. Our individual ability to adjust properly to changing price levels is what makes the changing level of prices either good or bad for each of us.

An investor who consistently buys low and sells high actually performs a social good. His buying in the face of panic selling supports the market and keeps it from going lower than might otherwise be the case; and his selling helps put a lid on a market advance, preventing the people who buy at market tops from paying even higher prices. At the same time he creates wealth that he can utilize to make life easier for himself while it leads to employment opportunities for others.

On the other hand, investors who buy in panic at market tops and sell at market bottoms help no one. They dissipate hard-earned wealth that might have been more productively spent. Such investors lose money that may have been needed for family living expenses, and add greater volatility to the stock market than is necessary. They thereby strain the efficient operation of the marketplace and encourage the adoption of legislation that invariably tends to calcify the market and make it less responsive to supply and demand.

50. Crowds

The Low-Risk Method works because of the tendency of people to become attracted to crowds. Whether it involves chasing a fire truck, rubbernecking at the scene of an accident or riot, going to a ball game or whatever, people like crowds. They like to be where the action is.

This is why volume moves up with prices during bull markets. As prices rise, more and more investors hear about the rise and become attracted to it. They want to be part of the action and taste the excitement of the moment.

This is what causes so many investors to get stuck in stocks right at the top. It is also responsible for the paradox that it is often easier for a seller to sell all his stock at the top than at any other price level. He can often sell thousands of shares here without causing more than a small ripple in the price pattern, because it seems that virtually everyone else is rushing to buy the stock.

Conversely, when a stock is dropping toward its final bottom, a shrewd investor can buy virtually all the stock he wants at the most advantageous prices. The same crowd, thoroughly frightened by this time, is rushing to sell and begging him to take the stock off their hands.

51. Emotional Triggers

People often delude themselves into thinking that all their decisions, investment and otherwise, are the result of intelligence and pure reason on their part. When things go wrong, therefore, the reason or the cause must be that a capricious and unpredictable world is conspiring against them. However, if they were to face themselves squarely and honestly, many investors would have to accept the inescapable conclusion that involuntary emotional patterns trigger them into action more often than they dare admit.

For instance, dark, gloomy, overcast, snowy, or rainy winter and spring days tend to depress many people with the result that if they think of the market at all, they probably think more of selling than of buying, regardless of whether this would be advantageous to them in the long run. If they are uncomfortable enough, their nervous system might well trigger their hand into reaching for the telephone and placing an order to sell stock. They would do the same thing on excessively humid days when their asthma attacks were coming on, or on summer days when an inversion of polluted air might cause widespread discomfort.

On clear, sunny, cool, crisp days, on the other hand, they would have more of a tendency to be optimistic, even in the face of a bear market when all purchases might best be avoided.   Personal difficulties, fights with friends or loved ones, problems at home or at work, illnesses, chance remarks are also often irrationally acted upon to the detriment of the investor. Such irrational emotional patterns often have a larger impact on the performance of many investors than any rational actions they might take.

52. The Need to Discharge Tensions

Many, perhaps most, investor decisions to buy or sell stocks do not come from logically derived decisions to buy or sell, but from an investor's need to get rid of an emotional build-up of some kind within his system. For example, someone might casually mention the name of a stock to an investor and not think any more about it. The investor becomes so interested in the stock that the only way he can stop thinking about it is to place an order to buy it. Or, he might for no apparent reason become concerned about a stock he already owns. As the days drag on, he finds he cannot shake off this fear in any way other than selling the stock.

Because of this, decisions to buy or sell stocks are often made, not so much because the outlook for a stock has suddenly changed dramatically, but because the investor had to do something to appease his tensions, his fears, his restlessness.

These tensions can arise not only from factors having to do with the relation of the investor to the stock market, but also from circumstances totally unrelated to the stock market. Without going into all the reasons that might trigger a stock-market transaction on the part of the investor, it is probably safe to generalize that it all boils down to his inability to make adequate or correct adjustments for what he sees happening in the world around him. Because of this inability to adjust quickly, the investor often suffers losses much greater than he has to.

As an example of how these emotional triggers work, take the case of a stock whose market has topped out and started to decline. Initially the investor has a profit. He does not therefore concern himself with this decline; he considers it merely a normal corrective action. There comes a time, however, when he recognizes the change in trend, but instead of selling, determines to wait for a rally.

When the rally does come the investor, instead of selling, lulls himself into thinking that it represents the beginning of a new bull market and decides to hold on. The price begins to recede again and the investor gets concerned once more, only to be lulled into inactivity by the next rally. With each drop, the tension inside the investor becomes greater until at some point it is so great that the only way it can be discharged and the investor's system be put to rest again is for him to sell his stock. The stronger willed or more insensitive the investor, the longer he will wait until he reaches the point where his pent-up internal pressure forces him to sell.

This is the drama, reenacted in countless numbers of persons at virtually the same time, that results in the buying and selling climaxes that so often characterize major turning points in the market.

These climaxes, therefore, are not the result of government policies or manipulations by others. In their simplest essence, they are the result of the inflexibility and unwillingness to take timely action on the part of large groups of investors acting independently when they first recognized that something was wrong with their investment programs. The losses they suffer as a result are due to their own actions and their own failures to act or refrain from acting at the proper times. In the case of panics, they hold back so long that their emotional forces finally compel them to act at the worst possible time.

Unfortunately, whenever such a battle between the will and the emotions occur within an investor, the emotions always seem to win.

Somehow the investor has to learn to act sooner, to sell as soon as he discovers that an error has been made. If he is losing money on the trade, he has to learn to overlook this loss because when he later sells in panic it will almost certainly be larger. He has to learn, too, to somehow stop being afraid. The Low-Risk System helps to eliminate such fear. Without fear to feed on, the investor rids his system of those personal conflicts that so often panic him into selling out right at the bottom.

53. The Proper Attitude Toward Money

Another important aspect of accumulation of wealth is a proper attitude toward money. We do not recommend a Pollyanna approach, but a confident, relaxed attitude appears mandatory if really large and worthwhile profits are ever to be achieved.

We have seen how, even though most stocks tend to go up and down together, there are occasions when stocks such as Brunswick display super growth tendencies, so strong that they are able to maintain a private uninterrupted bull market through several general-market bull-bear cycles. When they do occur, these extraordinary price moves offer investors an unbelievable opportunity to become wealthy. Just one such investment held to maturity is sufficient to wipe out the accumulated losses of many years. A big-enough investment in a super stock can make an investor wealthy for life.

Yet, it is probably safe to say that perhaps no more than a few dozen investors who owned Brunswick in the early 1950s realized even half the potential profit illustrated earlier. The rest either sold out too early or failed to sell at all until it was too late. It is also safe to say that only a handful of investors will ever realize fully the profits of the super stars yet to come. One reason, of course, is that until the publication of the Low-Risk Method most investors have not had adequate guidelines with which to measure the progress of their stocks. As a result, they have not known when to buy, how long to hold, or when to sell.

More important, however, most investors are not able to become sufficiently detached from their investments to allow them to mature properly. Instead they seem to combine a mixture of greed, fear, and duress that seldom allows their investments to mature properly. This appears to contradict an earlier statement about investors not caring about their investments, but while there is a contradiction in investor behavior patterns, there is no contradiction of the observations that were made.

It was noted that many investors are notoriously casual about the investment decisions they make. It was suggested that better results could be achieved if more concern was given to the decision-making process. Now the observation is offered that once an investor has made an initial decision, he tends to become overly concerned with performance. Instead of waiting patiently until the stocks fully mature to whatever level they are capable of, he expects too much from his stocks too quickly.

For example, an investor with a thousand dollars might decide he needs twice that amount for a specific purpose a year from now—by the fifth of next September, to be exact. As the examples in this book have shown, it is perfectly logical to expect a 100-percent return from many investments over a span of a year, providing the investor is willing to ride the tide of the market trend. But it is not logical to assume these returns can begin on any arbitrarily selected date and end on any pre-selected future date.

Initiating an investment on such a basis is as ludicrous as assuming an Iowa farmer could get an abundant harvest by planting a cornfield in mid-July, because he didn't have the time to prepare that particular field earlier in the year. The successful farmer knows that his bumper crops come only by the right combination of a willingness to work on his part, good seed (the right stocks), and planting at the proper season (a Low-Risk buy signal). After he has done all he can, there is nothing for the farmer to do but wait for his crop to mature (the High-Risk sell signal).

The problem with investors who cannot really afford to lose the money they are investing is that they work under pressures not conducive to either clear thinking or patience. Their fears and greed inhibit their chances for success and cause them to churn their portfolios too often and accept small profits even from their successful choices because in their fear, they are afraid to let any profit turn into a loss. On the other hand, they often allow losses to grow out of hand in the false hope that their judgment will somehow be vindicated.

54. Never Tell the Market What to Do

Never tell the market what to do. It doesn't want or need your opinion. Never try to work against the trend propelling the market at any given time. You cannot win.

No one, no matter how big he is or how wealthy he may be, is capable of successfully thumbing his nose at the force that propels the stock market, so it seems foolish for you to think you can. Some people seem to have the ability to manipulate the market, but all they ever really do is exaggerate whatever trend is in effect at any particular time. When the trend changes, if these people can't adapt themselves and cope with it, they will get wiped out. The more successful they seem to have been, the greater seems to be their fall.

Let the market tell you what to do. Become aggressive when the shadows it casts tell you that the risk is moderate. Be cautious and get out of the market when it tells you that the risk of being aggressive is high. Above all, be confident that, no matter how bad things seem to be, the day will come when there will be an opportunity to again make money.

55. One Cannot Know All Reasons Why Stocks Move

Nobody connected in any way with a stock or with the stock market, no matter how intimately, ever knows, ever can know, or ever will know all the reasons that even one stock moves in the direction and to the extent that it does. This is true because no one person can ever hope to track down and interview all the people who bought or sold any particular stock, or ever considered such transactions and then decid-ed not to go ahead with their trades.

Every decision to act, regardless of whether an investor buys or sells, and every decision to refrain from acting is in itself a force that has impact on the price of a stock. Because no one ever knows all the reasons why a stock moves, it becomes questionable whether he should make any inquiries about the reasons behind the movements of a stock. He might be better off assuming instead that the price of a stock at any particular moment is the ultimate resolution of all the forces that have any conceivable effect on that stock and let it go at that. By adopting such a viewpoint, an investor is less likely to be misled by the numerous reasons that can at any time be either irrelevant or misleading, and he will learn to train himself instead to always follow the trends of the stock.

The many reasons that may be given to explain the movements of stocks are very similar to the deceptions football teams practice against each other. Once you fully comprehend this, you can readily appreciate that the best advice to follow is: If you want to win the ball game, always keep your eye on the ball. Translated for the stock market, it reads: Keep your eye on the trend of the stock market and don't pay any attention to what is going on day by day, until the daily activity becomes persistent enough to change the direction of the trend.

56. Do Not Discuss Your Market Activities with Others

A stock-market rule observed much more in the breach than in observance is discussion of stock-market opinions and actions with others. As much as possible, it is wise, except when giving orders to a broker, to never discuss stock-market activities with anyone. This applies equally whether the discussion is initiated by you or by someone else.

There is something about verbalizing an idea that often makes it lose its effectiveness. A Low-Risk investor often reaches conclusions not shared by others. In the scheme of things, some of these ideas will be correct while some will be wrong. Either way, the investor may find himself embarrassed because he verbalized his thoughts.

If a person is wrong about an investment, it is rather easy to change one's mind in silence. Once someone else is aware of these ideas, however, especially if they in turn acted on them, it is difficult to abandon that path. Investors are continually being called upon to rationalize or defend ideas they might otherwise have discarded had no one known their position. Many people find their flexibility is inhibited when other people know what they are thinking.

On the other side of the coin, if you convince too many people of an idea before you yourself have acted on it, that idea may well lose its stock-market effectiveness because of the market's inability at times to accommodate too many people with the same idea at the same time.

57. Events Tend to Repeat Themselves

Earlier in the book, the historical tendency of the market to trace visible bottoms about every four years was discussed. It is well to fix this and similar repetitive patterns firmly in mind and to be prepared to act on them when the time for action arrives.

The mere knowledge that the stock market moves in cycles is not sufficient to insure that an investor will profit from this knowledge, because the reasons behind market moves differ from one cycle to the next. Most investors, therefore, remain convinced that the stock market does not move in cycles but in response to specific news events. In their attempt to adjust each stock-market wiggle to a specific news announcement, they lose sight of the repetitive nature of the moves themselves.

They completely miss market bottoms time after time because the auxiliary events that transpired and the sequence in which they occurred differ from one bottom to the next. They look for the same events to occur in exactly the same sequence in the future, but events don't repeat themselves in that way. Sometimes a few details will reappear unaccompanied by the main event, while at other times the principal event occurs unaccompanied by some of the details.

An example of one financial event that has repeated itself on a long-term cyclical basis is the phenomenon of unusually high interest rates. This has happened three times in the history of the country, each occurrence separated from the other by approximately 100 years. The first interest-rate peak took place in the 1770's during the Revolutionary War; the second peak, in the 1860's during the Civil War; and the third peak, during the late 1960's to end in mid-1970.

It is interesting to note that each peak coincided with what was in effect a "civil war" between major factions of the country. During the 1770's those Americans who were opting for a separation of the colonies from the mother country, England, fought against those who wanted to remain a colony of England. During the 1860's civil war flashed between those who wanted to practice the institution of slavery and those who wanted to abolish it. In the 1970's the latest peaks in interest rates have also been accompanied by what is in effect a civil war. Numerous apparently unrelated groups, in the name of numerous apparently unrelated causes, are demanding their "rights" to take to the street, instigate riots, destroy property, and otherwise assert their freedom to protest. After each previous period of disruption, weaknesses in the political and economic structure of the nation were discovered and strengthened and the nation moved on to new prosperity.

A knowledge of cyclical expectancies is a valuable aid to stock-market profits. The trick is to recognize those events that have a bearing on stock prices and to ignore the accompanying events and situations that distract investor attention from the broad tides in stock prices.

58. An Adequate Return on Investment is the Objective

An investor who refuses to take his losses gracefully ends up much like the shopkeeper who refuses to clear out all slow moving items. He ends up with a portfolio full of stale merchandise that becomes so old and shopworn that it cannot be sold except at a very substantial loss in price.

The best any investor can hope for in the market seems to be a profit ratio of about seven wins out of each ten attempts. Try to achieve this goal and be satisfied if and when you reach it. Anything else is unrealistic and almost impossible to attain. Beyond this, work to keep the three inevitable losses as small as possible. As soon as you recognize them, take them. Finally, the investor should try to build into himself the patience necessary to let those stocks that are working out well for him run as long as their trends are favorable, even if this means holding them for a much greater profit than he ever expected.

Remember, you only have to get rich once, but if you do it right and hold on to what you get, once is enough.

Summary

Here, in a nutshell, is what this book has tried to say.

It has tried to show that the struggle first to make consistent stock market profits and then to keep them is a dual struggle. On the one hand, the investor has to have an effective, dependable investment approach. On the other hand, he has to have confidence that his approach will indeed work. The investor needs to be patient in order to permit his investments to unfold their profit potential, and he needs to have discipline to keep from prematurely buying or selling stocks at times he knows are not advantageous for such actions.

To develop an investment approach, it was first necessary to determine what causes stocks to sell at any given level and what causes the level of prices to change. It was also necessary to observe the manner in which these changes occurred.

The reader saw that the price of a stock at any particular time was a composite of three factors. The first factor is the mathematically computed pro-rata share of the value of the company. This value can easily be computed except that different investors have different ideas of what should be included in this computation. Therefore, each person who makes such a computation is likely to arrive at a slightly different answer from that of someone else. But given a fixed hypothesis that an investor is willing to accept, it is possible to arrive at a precise value for a stock. This value will be relatively stable. It will change slowly and it will rarely be the price at which the stock is trading at any given time.

Modifying this basic price are a series of factors that have the effect of shifting the basic value either up or down from its originally computed sum. Among these are various combinations of political, economic, or industry-wide factors. A change in the level of interest rates, for instance, might shift the basic evaluation of an industry either up or down somewhat from the mathematically computed worth of a stock. The development of a new product might add to the value of an entire industry. At the same time it might cause a downward shift in an industry that was about to become obsolete. Here, too, any shifts once made tend to be relatively stable though not as stable perhaps as the basic shifts. Perhaps the price of a stock tends to trade closer to this adjusted value, but again, this value is rarely the price at which most stock transactions take place.

The investor who studies the price patterns stocks trace on charts over a period of time soon discovers that even when there seems to be little visible change in fundamental or shift factors, prices of most stocks swing over fairly wide arcs over a period of time. Furthermore, these swings occur in what often appear to be visible, regular, occasionally even predictable patterns covering extended periods of time sometimes lasting from six months to six years or more.

He also discovers that even with adjustments for political and other obvious factors, many stocks consistently trace their price swings above or below their adjusted values.

The student of these price patterns observes that prices of stocks are never stationary. They are always moving, sometimes above, and at other times below, some sort of invisible, imaginary normal value that is different and unique for each stock. Inquiry into the causes of this apparently irrational behavior eventually leads the investor to one conclusion: The most important, though least stable, determinate of stock prices lies initially in the changing attitudes of investors toward the stock, and then in the manner they translate this attitude into the buy-and-sell orders that affect the stock's market price.

To develop a successful investment approach then, an investor must find some way to measure and blend the shifting emphasis of fundamental, political, and emotional factors as they affect the price pattern at any particular time. He must find some way to determine which of many relevant factors has a bearing on the price pattern at the moment, and he must measure the effect of each factor vis-à-vis all other factors. Once he has accomplished this, he must still do two other things. He must find some means of determining the effect these factors will have on the probable future direction of prices, and he must find a way to pinpoint when major changes of attitude have occurred or are likely to occur.

The Low-Risk Method of Successful Investing described on the preceding pages meets these challenges simply and effectively. It does away with the difficulty of determining and assigning weights to these numerous factors by assuming that it is impossible for anyone to know which of the many variables will be of significance at any particular time; and that it is impossible to know precisely how much weight to assign each factor if it is known. Because these things are such unknowns, they are completely disregarded. Nevertheless, while it is impossible to know which factors have a bearing on the market at any time, the Low-Risk Method confidently proclaims it can measure the effect of these factors, providing the investor is willing to accept the premise that a stock's price at any moment in time is the ultimate resolution of all the factors and forces influencing it at that particular moment. If an investor can accept this premise, the Low-Risk Method proceeds to claim that he need focus on nothing else but price and the changing price pattern to determine what his investment position should be with respect to any stock at any time.

This book shows that it is mathematically possible to determine the early stages of every major change in market direction and to determine the price levels where purchases and sales can be made most advantageously. Furthermore, the techniques developed to capture these potentially available profits are simple and soundly grounded. They are designed so that an investor needs no mathematical skills beyond grade-school division to profitably employ the Low-Risk Method. The techniques contain only three elements, all easy to administer. They take very little time to compute and the answers they give are precise and nonambiguous. As a result, the investor is never in doubt as to the correct investment course to follow.

The three elements consist of the weekly closing prices of a small group of carefully pre-selected stocks, the weekly closing "price" of the Dow Jones industrial average, and the weekly cumulative difference in the number of stocks advancing in price versus those stocks that declined. It was found that focusing on just these three items out of the almost limitless number of available data yielded consistent superior results.

These various prices are used to construct a series of arithmetical moving averages that, when properly interpreted, measure the relative degree of risk or safety in the overall market. Then, within the context of this risk factor, the individual averages show the investor specifically when to buy and sell any stock in his pre-selected list. The averages themselves take very little time to maintain, only about a minute per stock per week.

These moving averages not only tell the investor what the market is doing but also what other investors as a group are thinking and doing. As we have seen, the level of stock prices is not merely a function of investment values but also a measure of investor attitudes. When the level of stock prices is rising, people become increasingly confident and enthusiastic; when it is falling, investors tend to become increasingly depressed, frightened, and susceptible to panic.

The Low-Risk Method works so effectively with so few elements because this changing price level is measured against the reference of a fixed period of time. When measured against such fixed time frames, the price of a stock generally moves up and down in alternate waves of expansion and contraction that can be both measured and anticipated.

Until the publication of this Low-Risk Method, there has never been available to the general investing public a method of investing so simple, so exact, or so reliable.

Unfortunately, possession of this method in itself is not sufficient to guarantee any investor consistent investment success. Even with the most reliable investment system available, the most important determinate of investment success or failure lies with each individual investor himself. It is possible that as much as 80 to 90 percent of an individual's investment success may be directly related to the manner in which he relates to the market at any particular time, and as little as 10 to 20 percent of his success is derived from his investment approach even though it is as reliable as the Low-Risk Method.

The investor must not only be able to anticipate major changes in market direction but he must also be able to make investment decisions that are in harmony with his anticipations. If he can do this, the investor is virtually guaranteed large and consistent investment profits. Although this book has conclusively demonstrated that it is mathematically possible to determine the early stages of major price advances, investors can, if they choose, make persuasive arguments for caution and the avoidance of making investments at such times. If they succeed, they will find it difficult or impossible to institute major buying programs at such Low-Risk periods, thus frustrating the effectiveness of their statistical efforts.

At the other extreme, the general market climate is sometimes so optimistic at market tops that, even when precise mathematical methods suggest selling, equally persuasive arguments can be made by an investor to minimize the impending danger. By not selling when given proper warning, the investor again frustrates the effectiveness of the Low-Risk Method.

Because of the importance the individual plays in his investment success, the second part of this book concentrated exclusively on individual and stock-market behavioral patterns. The objective here was to explain those patterns that both help and hinder the investor in his search for more consistent investment success. The examples were designed to show investors how they might work more effectively with, rather than against, the major market trends. Much of what was said is self-evident. But precisely because it is self-evident, these points are often either overlooked or not completely understood.

For example, it was noted that each investor brings into the market his own peculiar personality characteristics. These tend to individualize and differentiate him from all other investors. As a result, each investor views and reacts to the stock market differently. Each investor has different expectancies about the market. Each is attracted to or repelled by different stocks. Each places different weights and emphasis on whatever fundamental, economic, and political factors are influencing the market at any given time.

This brief paragraph explains why the personality make-up of some investors is such that it is possible for them to instinctively follow a course of action that is invariably profitable. Most investors are not so fortunate, however. Most investors have deficiencies of one kind or another that make investment success possible only with varying amounts of effort.

Most investors find themselves understandably diverted by the many irrelevancies and side issues that serve to confuse the investment picture. Such an investor, by following the Low-Risk Method, has the advantage of concentrating at regular weekly intervals on the true trend of the market as he computes the statistical data required by the method. While working on his computations, he gets to see precisely what the market is doing each week. This periodic concentration on the trend in time dissolves most of the confusion and indecision that confronts investors as a result of the conflicting reports about the market they consistently hear from brokers, advisers, the press, and others.

More than anything else, the Low-Risk Method develops confidence, discipline, patience, and coolness under pressure in the investor. An investor who gets unequivocable signals once each week for months on end to either hold or avoid a stock learns to be patient. As he sees these signals get him into stocks near their bottoms and sell him out near their tops, he develops sufficient discipline not to anticipate signals. Coolness under pressure comes most readily when the investor knows where he stands relative to all the extraneous factors that affect the market. Knowing what the stock market is doing inspires confidence. With confidence, fear is removed from the investment equation.

It is possible that there are better ways of selecting stocks than the Low-Risk Method. If so, they are unknown to the author. He knows of no system that is simpler or that works so well. The Low-Risk Method will work as long as prices continue to fluctuate and they always will.

Before closing, here is a summary of the Low-Risk Method market strategy that insures that every transaction an investor undertakes is done in harmony with the primary trend of the market.

1. Moving averages of the Dow Jones industrial average and the cumulative Advance-Decline line are relied on to indicate the primary-

trend direction of the general market.

2. Moving averages of individual stocks are relied on to indicate the primary-trend direction of individual stocks.

3. As soon as the general market turns up, after having been in a downtrend, Low-Risk strategy calls for becoming fully invested as quickly as possible.

4. At the time of a new bull market, the stocks to buy are chosen from among those that have given individual Low-Risk buy signals immediately prior to the general market upturn. By turning up early, these stocks are displaying the necessary relative strength to become the leaders of the coming bull market.

5. As long as the general market trend is up, the strategy is to remain fully invested.

6. When *either* the DJI or A-D indexes turn down, the future trend is uncertain. At such times, further purchases of stocks are deferred until the market picture clarifies. Stocks already in a portfolio, however, are not to be sold except in accordance with the rules for selling stocks in uncertain periods.

7. When *both* the DJI and A-D indexes turn down, a bear market is presumed to be in effect. At such times no purchases are to be made. Stocks already in a portfolio are to be sold only in accordance with the rules for selling in a bear market.

We've tried to show that it is possible for every investor to succeed in the stock market. We've tried to give you the confidence to do for yourself something that no one else has been able to do for you before. We've tried to show that it is not difficult to achieve consistent stock-market success but to achieve it you must work at it, not hard, not much, but you must work nevertheless. If you exercise a little bit of common sense and self-restraint, the market is not nearly as formidable as people have told you it was.

By following the rules in this book, you will learn that making money in the stock market is easier than losing it ever was. You now know how to go about it. All you need to do is start. Good Luck!

ADDENDUM

Since this book was first published, many people have written to say that when the book was revised, it should contain detailed instructions for setting up individual work sheets as well as for adjusting the sheets for stock splits and dividends. For those who find this information useful, the following schedules might be helpful.

Appendices

APPENDIX A

SETTING UP A MASTER INVESTMENT LIST

How Many Stocks Should You Follow?

The primary consideration in setting up a Master Investment List comes down to the amount of time a person has to spend on his investments. The more time a person has for this project or the more money he has to invest, the more stocks can be included in such a list. If less time is available, fewer stocks need be kept.

Within this framework, the least number of stocks that it makes sense to follow is 25 while the maximum number for most people is 200.

Whatever number you decide on, don't try to construct your Master List all at once. Start slow because then if you should decide this system is not for you, your investment of time will have been kept to a minimum. It's best to start with somewhere between 10 and 25 stocks at first.

See if you are comfortable with the system and learn to make the work involved in updating your work sheets each week as automatic as possible. Remember that with practice your proficiency will increase. With increased proficiency it may not take you much longer to do 100 stocks after six months that it took you to do 25 stocks the first week.

The warning to go slow actually serves two functions. It lets you "debug" your routines as the computer people say. That is, it lets you work out your mistakes while you are still working on a small scale.

Second, it keeps you from getting discouraged in the beginning because you are taking too much time.

Do not begin to add any new stocks to your list until you are working quickly and easily with your first few stocks. Only then should you add to this first group of stocks a little at a time until the list is up to the size you want it. Five new stocks a week is more than enough.

What materials do you need?

1. A supply of lined columnar paper with at least seven columns.

2. A calculator. It doesn't have to be fancy just so it can do the basic calculations of addition, subtraction and division. For your purposes a $10 calculator is every bit as good as a programable calculator that costs $1,000 or more. Both will give you the same answers. The most important thing to keep in mind is the ease and comfort in using it. Before you buy a calculator try working some problems on a few calculators and buy the one whose keyboard is most comfortable for your touch.

3. Some kind of source document from which to extract the stock prices for the past 40 weeks. This can include . . .

   a. Stock tables accumulated from the Sunday edition of your newspaper for the past 40 weeks. You can also use the Monday edition of the Wall Street Journal or Barron's Magazine.

   b. A chart book which shows the closing prices for each week. We show the 3-Trend Security Charts from Securities Research Co. in this book but there are probably a dozen other services whose charts you can use if you prefer.

   c. A hard cover publication called the ISL Index. This is issued quarterly and lists in one column the daily price range for each stock for a full 13 week period. Separate volumes are published for the New York Stock Exchange, the Amex and the O-T-C market. This is the best publication to use because it is the most convenient. But it is extremely expensive for your needs. However check with your broker or your library and if they have this reference try to borrow it.

What Stocks to Follow

1. First and most important construct work sheets for every stock you currently own.

2. Next take a few stocks from the master investment list beginning on page 58.

3. Pick a few of your own stocks after reviewing

   a. A long range chart book, or

   b. A monthly Stock Guide or Stock Digest available from your broker or

   c. Publications from the stock exchanges showing the stocks listed on them.

4. Finally, if you must, if someone gives you a tip that sounds too good to be true, do a work sheet on it before you rush out to buy.

APPENDIX B

CONSTRUCTING A WORK SHEET

Let's assume you are all set to begin constructing your work sheets. Here's what you do.

First take a sheet of columnar paper and head it as you see the Trans World Airlines work sheet set up on page 114.

If the paper you are using doesn't have enough columns to include all the headings, you can eliminate the "Take Away Price" columns and put the check off marks instead to the immediate left of the 5 - 15 and 40 week total prices. This will leave you with a seven column work sheet that looks like this:

	5 Week		15 Week		40 Week	
Price	Total	Average	Total	Average	Total	Average

Next take the source data that you are going to work with. For this example, we are going to construct a work sheet for Dr. Pepper Co. using as our source the weekly stock chart from 3-Trend Security Charts.

1. Before starting count down to line 25 of the "Price" column on the work sheet and put a small check mark at the far left or right of the price column. Do the same thing on lines 35 and 40.

2. Next look at the Dr. Pepper chart.(Figure 37) Go to the weekly price range at the far right of the chart. This is the most recent price range of the stock for the week ending April 23, 1976. That week the stock sold as low as 14½ and as high as 15⅞. From this line pick the closing price for the week. The closing price is shown by the heavy horizontal bar just a little above 15½. Since this bar is about ¼ the distance between 15½ and 16, we estimate the closing price for the week was 15⅝.

3. If, instead of the chart, you are working from a newspaper you simply use the actual "Last" price for April 23 as posted in your paper.

4. Now enter this closing price of 15⅝ on line 40 of the "Price" column on your work sheet.

5. From line 40 you work backward. Take the closing price for the next to the last week on the chart. This is immediately to the left of 15⅝ and happens to be 14½. Post 14½ on line 39 of the price column.

6. Keep doing this working up on your work sheet and left on the chart (15, 16¼, 15½, 15⅞, 16, 16½, etc.) until all 40 spaces on your work sheet have been filled. Don't worry if you should post a price incorrectly by an eighth or quarter of a point occasionally because all your plus and minus errors will probably balance each other out. The important thing to remember is this is a fast way to get your work sheets completed. If you have a small error but post your weekly update prices correctly, in a few weeks the error will resolve itself.

7. After you have posted all 40 prices on your work sheet, take out

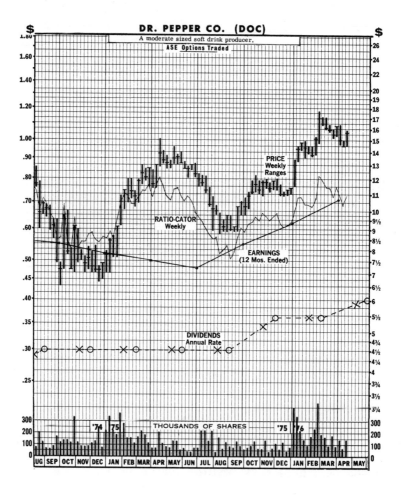

Figure 37

your calculator and add the prices from lines 36 through 40. Put this answer (76⅞) on line 40 in the 5-Week Total column. At the same time put a check mark or an "X" on line 35. This tells you that the 76⅞ total was obtained from the prices which came after line 35.

8. Leave the 5-Week total (76.875) in your calculator and continue adding to that total the prices on lines 26 through 35. Post this total (228½) on line 40 in the 15-Week Total column. At the same time put a check mark or an "X" on line 25 in the 15-Week Total column.

9. Retain the 15-Week total (228.50) in your computer and add the prices from lines 1 through 25. Post this total (497) on line 40 in the 40-Week Total column.

10. Divide the 40-Week Total (497.00) by 40. The answer is 12.425. Round this off to two places and post 12.43 to the 40-Week Average column on line 40.

11. Go back to the 5-Week Total (76.875) and divide it by 5. The answer is 15.375. Round the answer to 15.38 and post it to the 5-Week Average column.

12. Finally enter the 15-Week Total (228½) in your computer and divide by 15. The answer will be 15.2333 +. Post 15.23 to the 15-Week Average column.

That's all there is to it. Line 40 shows the current price of Dr. Pepper is 15⅝; the 5-Week Average, 15.38; 15-Week Average 15.23; and 40-Week Average 12.43. If you own the stock you should hold and if you are looking to buy you would wait until the price dropped to between 15.23 and 12.43.

Your work sheet is now complete and ready to update each week. If you did it correctly, it will look like this:

DR. PEPPER CO.

Price	5 week Total	Average	15 week Total	Average	40 week Total	Average
10⅜						
10⅛						
10						
9¼						
9⅛						
9¾						
9						
9⅛						
10¼						
10½						
10¼						

Price	5 week Total	5 week Average	15 week Total	15 week Average	40 week Total	40 week Average
10⅞						
11⅛						
11⅝						
11¼						
11¾						
11¾						
11⅜						
11⅞						
11½						
11						
11						
11¼						
11⅜						
13	x		x			
14¼						
14¾						
14⅜						
14						
13¾						
15⅛						
17						
16½						
16						
15⅞	x	x				
15½						
16¼						
15						
14½						
15⅝	x 76⅞	15.38	228½	15.23	497	12.43

On the following week, April 30 when you update Dr. Pepper for the first time, here is all you do.

1. Post the Friday April 30 closing price of 15⅛ to column 1.

2. Take last week's 5-Week Total of 76⅞ and enter it in your computer. Then add this week's price (15⅛) and subtract the price 5 weeks ago (15½) and press the (=) button to get your updated 5-Week Total. Post this number (76½) to Column 2 and at the same time put a check mark on line 36 to show that you have used the 5-Week price from that line.

3. Divide 76½ by 5 to get your updated 5-Week Average (15.30) and post it to Column 3.

4. Do the same thing to your 15-Week Total from Column 4. Add 15⅛ to 228½, then subtract 14¼. The new total is 229⅜ which is posted to Column 3 with a check mark back on line 26.

5. Divide 229⅜ by 15 and post this new 15-Week Average (15.29) to Column 5.

6. Do the same thing with the 40 Week Total. The new updated total is 501¾. The check mark goes on line 1 and the revised 40 Week Average of 12.54 is posted to Column 7.

Once you get this routine set in your mind to the point where it is automatic, it will take you far less time to make your computations than it did to read about it here.

To be sure that you understand how this works, the work sheet has been updated for several more weeks. Update each week's prices on your calculator and double check your answers against this example before going on to prepare any work sheets on your own.

DR. PEPPER CO.

Price	5 week Total	5 week Average	15 week Total	15 week Average	40 week Total	40 week Average
10⅜					x	
10⅛					x	
10					x	
9¼					x	
9⅛					x	
9¾					x	
9					x	
9⅛					x	
10¼					x	
10½						
10¼						
10⅞						
11⅛						
11⅝						
11¼						
11¾						
11¾						
11⅜						
11⅞						
11½						
11						
11						
11¼						
11⅜						
13	x		x			
14¼			x			
14¾			x			
14⅜			x			
14			x			

Price	5 week Total	5 week Average	15 week Total	15 week Average	40 week Total	40 week Average
13¾			x			
15⅛			x			
17			x			
16½			x			
16			x			
15⅞ x x						
15½ x						
16¼ x						
15 x						
14½ x						
15⅝ x x	76⅞	15.38	228½	15.23	497	12.43
15⅛ x	76½	15.30	229⅜	15.29	501¾	12.54
14⅝ x	74⅞	14.98	229¼	15.28	506¼	12.66
14⅝ x	74½	14.90	229½	15.30	510⅞	12.77
14⅜ x	74⅜	14.88	229⅞	15.33	516	12.90
13⅞	72⅝	14.53	230	15.33	520¾	13.02
13¼	70¾	14.15	228⅛	15.21	524¼	13.11
14	70⅛	14.03	225⅛	15.01	529¼	13.23
16⅜	71⅞	14.38	225	15.00	536½	13.41
16¼	73¾	14.75	225¼	15.02	542½	13.56

APPENDIX C

STOCK SPLITS

The one problem that seems to have evoked more letters from readers than anything else is what to do when a company splits its stock. Some people found the question so confusing that they wanted to stop following any stock that had a split.

Nothing that drastic need be done because the adjustment for a stock split is actually quite simple. All you have to do is first adjust the most current 5-week; 15-week and 40-week totals to reflect the split. Then do the same thing to the week-end stock prices for the past 40 weeks.

For example let's say that a stock has split 2 for 1. What this means is that after the split an investor in the stock will have twice as many shares but each share will only be worth half as much. So to adjust your work sheet you have to make every significant number half as big as before.

We may have a work sheet that looks like this. (The columns we don't do anything with are excluded in this example.)

Price	5-week Total	15-week Total	40-week Total
97¾	488.75	1455.50	4456.75
95¼	489.75	1456.50	4457.50
96⅝	490.00	1458.25	4458.25
104	494.50	1458.75	4460.00
102⅛	495.75	1460.25	4461.75

Since the stock will only be worth half as much after the split, we divide the most current 5 week total by 2 and get an adjusted 5 week total of 247.875; the adjusted 15 week total is 730.125; and the 40 week total is 2230.875. We cross out the old totals and put these corrected prices beside them on the line below. Then we do the same thing for all 40 week end closing prices. When we are finished our work sheet will look like this.

Price	5-week Total	15-week Total	40-week Total
48⅞	488.75	1455.50	4456.75
47⅝	489.75	1456.50	4457.50

Price	5-week Total	15-week Total	40-week Total
48.3123	490.00	1458.25	4458.25
52	494.50	1458.75	4460.00
51.0625 (adj for 2/1 split)	247.88	730.13	2230.88
51¼	250.75	730.38	2231.13

After making the adjustments go on in the same way as you did before. All the relationships between the 5 - 15 and 40 week moving averages will stay the same, the signals will also stay the same. Nothing will change except that all the numbers are now half as big as they were before.

To determine how much to divide by when adjusting for a split, here is the formula to follow: number of new shares divided by the number of old shares equals the diviser or the number to divide by.

Here is a handy table to save you time in adjusting for the more common splits.

If a split is	then divide by
2 for 1	2
3 for 1	3
4 for 1	4
3 for 2	1.5
5 for 4	1.25
1 for 2	.5
1 for 3	.333
1 for 4	.25
1 for 5	.20

Remember, it isn't necessary to adjust every number on your work sheet, only the prices for the past 40 weeks and the most recent 5 - 15 and 40 week totals for the week immediately prior to the split.